Purposeful Writing

Genre Study
in the Secondary
Writing Workshop

Rebecca Bowers Sipe
Tracy Rosewarne

HEINEMANN
Portsmouth, NH

Heinemann
A division of Reed Elsevier Inc.
361 Hanover Street
Portsmouth, NH 03801–3912
www.heinemann.com

Offices and agents throughout the world

The authors and publisher wish to thank those who have generously given permission to reprint borrowed material:

"The Butterfly" by Pavel Friedman from *I Never Saw Another Butterfly* by U.S. Holocaust Memorial Museum, edited by Hana Volavkova. Copyright © 1978, 1993 by Artia, Prague. Compilation © 1993 by Schocken Books. Used by permission of Schocken Books, a division of Random House, Inc.

"Terezin" from *I Never Saw Another Butterfly* by U.S. Holocaust Memorial Museum, edited by Hana Volavkova. Copyright © 1978, 1993 by Artia, Prague. Compilation © 1993 by Schocken Books. Used by permission of Schocken Books, a division of Random House, Inc.

"Naked" from *Chicks Up Front* by Sara Holbrook. Copyright © 1998. Published by Cleveland State University Poetry Center. Reprinted by permission of the publisher.

Acknowledgments for borrowed material continue on p. viii.

Library of Congress Cataloging-in-Publication Data
Sipe, Rebecca Bowers.
  Purposeful writing : genre study in the secondary writing workshop / Rebecca Bowers Sipe and Tracy Rosewarne.
    p. cm.
  Includes index.
  ISBN-13: 978-0-325-00955-1
  ISBN-10: 0-325-00955-4
  1. English language—Study and teaching (Secondary). 2. English language—Composition and exercises—Study and teaching (Secondary). I. Rosewarne, Tracy. II. Title.
LB1631.S5155 2006
808′.0420712—dc22   2006019534

Editor: James Strickland
Production management: Denise Botelho
Production coordination: Vicki Kasabian
Cover design: Night and Day Design
Typesetter: House of Equations, Inc.
Manufacturing: Steve Bernier

Printed in the United States of America on acid-free paper
10 09 08 07 06 EB 1 2 3 4 5

Contents

Acknowledgments

This book and the questions that prompted it belong to many people, and we owe all of them special thanks for helping us as we set about sharing this story. Without a doubt, it was the support and assistance of Jim Strickland, our editor and friend, that made this book a reality. Not only is Jim a terrific editor, he is the best cheerleader a writer could have. He and Kathleen Strickland have offered encouragement and assistance every step of the way, and Vicki Kasabian, our production editor, has worked tirelessly to help create a book that will be useful to other teachers.

A special debt is owed the students of Community High School. What an amazing group of young people! At Community, students, faculty, and Dean Judy work together everyday to create a unique and energizing learning environment that stands as an example of what is working in secondary education. To Tracy's students who participated in this project and to Ellen Stone and Chris Erickson who helped make the class possible, we offer our deepest appreciation.

Heartfelt thanks go to Kathleen Rowlands and Jim Mahoney who gave graciously of their time to offer both encouragement and suggestions. And, to our colleagues and friends in the Eastern Michigan Writing Project who have shaped our thinking in so many different ways, we offer our own encouragement to remember that the questions we have about our classrooms matter. In this day of political and external pressure facing every local classroom, it is tremendously important to tell our stories about real classrooms, real students, and highly effective practices that make sense.

Finally, to those who know us best—to Michael, Dera, and Justin and to Brian, Sophia, and Ella—thank you all for allowing us to carve out time to grow as teachers. You have our love, appreciation, and gratitude.

Rebecca and Tracy

Introduction

*I really enjoyed the writing we did in your workshop, but for high
school kids, basically I think that stuff's all whipped cream.*
                            —Anonymous, department chair

The workshop in question, cosponsored by the Eastern Michigan Writing Project
and the North Central Association (EMWP/NCA) as a part of a full-day writing
session for teachers and principals, provided a quick foray into memoir writing.
Together, we read *Wilfrid Gordon McDonald Partridge* by Mem Fox, talked about
special memories the story evoked for us, created individual chains of memories,
and then each of us chose one memory to work with for a few minutes.

But, we didn't just jump in. First, we dropped ourselves into the memory by
visualizing the episode: who was a part of the event? What sensory images did the
memory include? We sketched a rough picture based on the memory and then
told the story to an individual seated nearby. In a few cases, the stories were shared
with the larger group and we used them, as well as the picture book, to think together about the qualities a memoir might have, drawing on other memoirs of
which participants were familiar. And then we wrote: words rapidly flowed onto
paper.

As I walked around the room, I observed writers scratching out words to substitute better ones. I noticed loopy lines inserted to move phrases to better loca-
tions in fastwrites. I saw writers pausing, thinking, and then lurching forward again
with a new burst of energy. The most exciting thing I noted, however, happened
after I interrupted the writing to see if anyone was willing to share. In a room filled
with strangers an hour earlier, hands went up in all directions as adult writers
eagerly shared their stories.

Certainly the brief simulation the participants experienced did not provide
for immersion in the genre. It did, however, provide a platform for us to talk about
and experience, however briefly, some of the things that support us as writers when
we jump into a new genre. We talked about the need to experience the genre so
that we could get a sense of its possibilities and its restrictions. Sometimes scaffolding is needed to help us create a mental model of the genre: How is it organized? What about the author's stance in this type of writing? What about various

elements of style? And, sometimes we need interactions with texts or peers to whet our appetites and help us think about the story, message, or information we want to share.

I listened hard to the department chair as he stood before me describing a new approach he had developed and was teaching to others in his district, a more prescriptive approach than the one we had discussed in our workshop, one that privileged organization and mechanics as essential features students should master before concentrating on other elements—like content, voice, and audience. He described how unprepared teachers, and particularly new teachers, are to address the requirements of academic writing, and how the set of principles he had developed could be taken successfully into any genre and guarantee well-organized results.

I listened with a knitted brow, my mind filled with a rush of thoughts, and I struggled with the suggestion that academic writing could be boiled down to such a narrow notion of genre. Genre suggests categories, and in the world of experienced writers, clean-cut categories are hard to find. All writing takes on a persuasive element, and good writing of all types may exhibit deep descriptions, strong voice, and manipulation of conventional rhetorical structures. Some genres blend into others; some open up to numerous subgenres. Even in traditional academic genres like the essay, crisp genre-based definitions have become blurred and variations including multigenre presentations written for traditional purposes are commonplace.

Certainly, I believed in the importance of immersion in and exploration of unfamiliar genres as gateways to understanding their various possibilities, restraints, and conventions. My experience told me, however, that the most important thing of all is having something that needs to be captured in print. When writers have something important to say, they are more apt to care about all those qualities that help a reader understand and appreciate the message. They have a context for the importance of qualities such as clear organization and appropriate mechanics.

Too often, I fear, writing in school fails to account for the crucial need authors have for purpose and relevance, and that without these, writing itself may seem only an academic exercise for young adults, an exercise unworthy of much effort or concern. The disconnect that many students feel for school-sponsored writing reinforces their sense that school-based writing is an academic exercise, one for which learning formulaic patterns for sentence and paragraph placement is what writing is all about. If young adults are to develop writing identities and a sense of the importance of their words, ideas, and opinions, they need more than a formula.

Robert Yagelski (2000) thoughtfully describes how critical it is to help our students understand that their voices matter if we want them to believe that writing has relevance in their lives. There are many in our field who offer visions for how this may be done. Jay Robinson (1998), for example, urges us to create habitable spaces in schools, spaces where students can experience a connection between school-sponsored literacy and the discourses that matter in the world. Describing partnership projects such as the Saginaw River Project, which engaged students from two high schools in the real work of testing and reporting on water quality, he shares how such a project created a context for writing that significantly affected a community. For the students involved, clearly writing mattered because it had a real purpose, audience, and message, and it offered the possibility of making a difference. Because it offered these elements, it warranted the time to carefully consider organization, word choice, and conventions.

Like Yagelski and Robinson, who powerfully describe why purpose and context are so essential for the development of writing that matters, I contend that before students will be concerned about organization, format, and mechanics they must first have something to say and a reason to say it. By situating writing instruction among conversations focused on things that matter, conversations fueled by broad reading of fiction and nonfiction literature, students will not only have something to think about, they will also be more likely to develop ideas they want and need to share. Unless we have something to say, why worry about organization and correctness?

The department chair's concerns for his students were evident, predictable, and heartfelt. Teachers everywhere recognize that young adults face numerous expectations for writing on demand, he explained, at school, on writing tests to exit high school, and on writing tasks at work and in college. In his mind, organization and mechanics were top priorities for these students. After all, writing that is poorly organized, that does not honor basic constraints of genre, and of expectations for correctness in spelling, capitalization, and punctuation is apt to be relegated to the bottom of the heap regardless of the significance of the message intended.

He is not alone in the concerns he voices. Faced with heavy curricular expectations and testing requirements, many teachers struggle with questions of how best to approach the teaching of writing. Certainly, the question of how best to do that was the backdrop to the EMWP/NCA workshop conversation, and it continues to be important in our ongoing national conversations as well. How *do* we most effectively prepare students for the writing tasks they encounter in school and beyond as they assume their responsibilities and exercise their rights within a democratic society? How do we do so while helping them see the relevance to their own lives? How do we do so within an academic framework that is engaging, challenging, and rigorous? How do we create learning spaces and moments that meet the needs of radically diverse high school students? Can we even teach writing in any sort of didactic fashion?

"Can we teach writing?" That is the opening question in Donald Murray's *Write to Learn* (1984). He answers his own question: "Yes, but we can't teach writing in advance of our students writing. Our students do not learn to write, then write . . ." (xiii). Implicit is the understanding that our students learn to write best when they are actually engaged in meaningful writing experiences. This premise has provided a rich focus for professional conversations at the elementary and middle school levels where teachers such as Katie Wood Ray (2004), Regie Routman (1991, 1988), Nancie Atwell (1987, 1998), Donald Graves (1994), and Linda Rief (1992), among others, have described successful workshop environments where students spend the majority of their class time actually doing those things that we value—reading real literature and using that as an inspiration for writing real texts.

Richard Bullock (1998), working with ten teachers from middle and high schools, articulates the features of a high school workshop classroom and identifies many of the obstacles teachers face as they attempt to create workshops for their students.

Traditional environments	Workshop environments
The teacher (or school or state) designs and implements the curriculum.	Teacher and students negotiate curriculum, both individually and in groups (within mandated constraints).
Students practice skills and memorize facts.	Students actively construct concepts and meanings.
Content is broken down into discrete, sequential units.	Content is presented whole, in meaningful contexts.
Avoiding mistakes is important.	Taking risks is valued as a sign of learning.
Performance on tests is valued highly.	Students are assessed by their performance on meaningful tasks, often through portfolios of their work.
Teachers do the evaluating and grading.	Students learn to assess their own learning and progress.
Learning is expected to be uniform. Expectations are the same for all students, so many students "fail."	Learning is expected to be individual and unique. Evaluation is oriented toward success.

Unlike the classroom where structure and format are privileged first, the workshop environments described by Sheridan Blau (2003), John Gaughan (2001), and Kathleen Andrasick (1990) provide an opportunity for students to immerse themselves in literature, using individual and whole group texts as platforms for talking and writing about ideas—big ideas and smaller ideas that are also personally and locally relevant. Then, given opportunities to examine the distinctive features of the texts being read, students have the opportunity to develop mental models for specific genres. They are afforded the opportunity to ask important questions such as when and why a writer would choose memoir or short story or persuasive essay as the *best* tool for relaying her message? What features of a particular genre make it the best one for a particular purpose? What are the possibilities inherent in a particular genre choice? What restrictions for shaping the message would it require? In this classroom, genre becomes a tool for a writer's message and sculpts decisions about organization, mechanics, and other rhetorical concerns. In this classroom, writers hold power to make decisions about how their messages will be transmitted.

The publication of *The Neglected R* by the National Commission on Writing in America's Schools and Colleges (2003) reinforced for the nation the importance of writing in our lives and in our schools. Asserting that "[w]riting today is not a frill for the few, but an essential skill for the many" (11), the report goes on to describe writing as "not simply a way for students to demonstrate what they know . . . [but] a way to help them understand what they know. At best, writing is learning" (13). This important document goes on to report that high school students experience few opportunities to produce thoughtful—and thought filled—papers in a variety of genres written for varying purposes and audiences. The commission urges schools to place writing at the center of the curriculum, to engage students in writing often and in a variety of contexts. It also urges legislators and policy makers to find resources to support teachers in this critical enterprise.

The Neglected R is certainly not alone in recognizing the critical place writing holds in supporting students as communicators and thinkers. For many years professional organizations such as the National Council of Teachers of English and the National Writing Project have advocated increasing the amount of instructional time devoted to writing. The recently released *NCTE Beliefs About the Teaching of Writing* (2004, see Appendix A), resulted in eleven broad statements supporting particular practices in relation to the teaching of writing, representing a synthesis of research, K–16. These principles include support for writing process and the teaching of writing through actual writing practice.

Devoting enormous effort to sift through a mountain of reform reports and standards projects, Daniels, Zemelman, and Hyde (1998, 1993) synthesized a list of qualities that have come to be known as characteristics of "best practices" for instruction. These principles call for classrooms that are "student-centered, experiential, reflective, authentic, holistic, social, collaborative, democratic, cognitive, developmental, constructivist, [and] challenging" (4–5). These authors go on to describe a series of shifts away from certain practices and toward others, including a movement toward experiential, inductive, hands-on learning; more active learning; more emphasis on higher-order thinking; more choice and more collaborative activity. In addition, this meta-study made recommendations for "six structures that help create Best Practice classrooms," including use of "integrative units, small group activities, representing-to-learn, classroom workshop, authentic experiences, [and] reflective assessment" (5).

I have had opportunities to ask many teaching colleagues around the country to think about that moment when they first knew they were a reader, that magic time when they were so absorbed in a story that they were living within the pages, experiencing that "moment of unconscious delight" (161–67) described by Margaret Early (1960) as an essential step toward literary appreciation. Without it, she cautions, readers will lack the investment and skill to handle higher levels of literary analysis in meaningful ways. When I ask these same colleagues to describe that moment when they first truly felt they were a writer, many confess that they have no such recollection—that even as adults they do not see themselves as writers. Why would this be?

Perhaps writing, like reading, requires that moment of unconscious delight, that moment when we are so engaged in our message that we are not only willing but excited about investing energy and effort to make it reflect our experience perfectly—to make it just right for a reader. Surely students can have such moments as they work with a variety of genres, but only if the writing itself has meaning and significance. When a high school writer has something to say, word choice, mechanics, sentence structure, and organization have a purpose. When the reading and writing are compelling, a bridge is opened for the teacher to point to ways a writer uses conventions, word choice, and organization as deliberate tools—tools that students can make their own for immediate use to convey their own messages.

That's what workshop at the high school level is all about—purposeful reading and writing to promote engagement with ideas and to create environments where young writers sculpt their understanding of genre, craft, and skills because they are important to the message they wish to convey. This is an organic approach, one that mirrors the way adult writers approach new and unfamiliar writing tasks. This is understanding the demands of the writing task from the inside, and no prescription can give that intuitive sense of the work.

No Prescriptions Necessary

This book grows from the premise that we don't need prescriptive approaches and environments to teach writing and that, in fact, such approaches may be at cross-purposes to our long-term goals for writing. In the pages that follow, I will invite the reader to join me as I enter the classroom of a magnificent teacher, Tracy

Rosewarne. At a very fundamental level, Tracy and I believe that the qualities of a workshop environment create a more successful pedagogical structure for supporting the growth of adolescent writers than any other model. If students learn to work effectively in a variety of genres selected for varying purposes and audiences, if they understand the power of their own words, and if they sense the responsibilities associated with putting their thoughts and words into the world, surely they will be better prepared for whatever writing demands—including demands of testing—come their way.

As a teacher of preservice students, I have often encountered the question, "Couldn't someone just show me what writing workshop looks like at high school?" Preservice students frequently raise questions about classroom management and about how teachers manage to fit in everything they are suppose to teach. This book is written with these questions in mind. Its purpose is twofold. The first is to provide a context for understanding the ways an excellent teacher negotiates the very complex demands placed on the high school instructional setting—demands emanating from national and state standards and testing, from local curriculum requirements, and from a teacher's keen understanding of best practices and strong sense of professional responsibility. The second purpose is to offer a picture of workshop in a diverse, urban, block-scheduled high school classroom. In doing so we examine the ways Tracy honors her core beliefs—the foundation of her workshop even in more teacher-directed units—and by doing so creates relevance, builds relationships, and designs rigorous learning opportunities.

In the following pages, we trace the development of an actual writing workshop by looking closely at the ways in which community and expectations are established; we then turn a sharp lens on two representative units, one focused on exploration of nonfiction genres and the second dedicated to open student choice of reading and writing. In both cases students write in genres and on topics of their own choosing, though in the first unit, the genre choices are limited to nonfiction. In later chapters, we look closely at classroom essentials, like the writer's notebook. We give details about how Tracy set up her workshop; how she addressed the multitude of curricular requirements that confronted her and her students; and how she wove in essential instruction through mini- and microlessons, drawing out for scrutiny essential skills and encouraging students to immediately embed them into their thinking and writing through skills and craft lessons. We document the ways in which the workshop was successful and discuss variations that may be considered.

In particular, we discuss ways in which student attitudes about writing changed and how their proficiency as writers grew. Throughout, we include examples of student writing, instructional plans, and model lessons to support thinking and planning for workshops. Finally, to support the development of workshop environments in other high school classrooms, we include in an appendix two important classroom tools for copying or modifying. We do not provide a cookie cutter model. Instead, our goal is to open up conversation for sharing multiple visions of successful workshops that support reading and writing at the high school level.

—RBS

Part 1

• • • • • •

A Community of Learners

Establishing a sense of community is essential if students are to engage in the hard work of writing in a workshop environment. Workshop means taking risks with new types of writing, pushing the limits to think about one's own writing with new eyes. It means taking ownership and responsibility for one's own writing voice and identity, and taking responsibility for supporting the growth of others.

Tracy works throughout the semester to support a sense of community among her students. The first two days, however, are critical for helping students sense how connected they are in the workshop and how important they will be to one another's growth. During these first two days, she establishes a system in which students will change groups daily. This system provides a platform for working with many different students in the class. Students learn about giving and receiving responses to their writing, and that regardless of their confidence in their writing, they can both offer support to another writer and benefit from the insights of each of their response partners. By immediately establishing a predictable system for working in groups, offering responses, and using feedback in productive ways, students begin to develop trust and security on the very first day of the semester.

During Days One and Two, students write and respond continuously. Activities pull them together as a group as they share personal stories about writing, learn about one another's fears and concerns, and come to understand the many ways they are connected—an understanding that makes it clear that every action by every student affects the group in fundamental ways.

1

A Framework for Learning

"All right," Tracy said with intensity, "what do writers really need?"

On a sweltering day in July, Tracy and I duck into our favorite Mexican restaurant. Within minutes the placemats are flipped to provide white space for the notes that follow. "All right," says Tracy with intensity, "what do writers *really* need?" We had reread Atwell (1987, 1991) and Rief (1992), and are cofacilitating a summer intensive workshop focused on the works of Louise Rosenblatt (1938, 1976), a workshop that helped a dozen educators apply Rosenblatt's transactional reading theory—a theory that describes meaning as a personal act, one resulting from the transaction of a reader and a text—to the teaching of writing. This day these influences provide a context that shapes our thinking about the workshop Tracy hopes to create for her high school students.

We know that Tracy's school provides a unique setting in several ways. Because it is a school of choice, it draws students from across a highly diverse community in Michigan. In addition to cultural diversity, the school also comprises a population of widely differing learning needs. Tracy's school utilizes a block schedule—a potential advantage for a workshop because of the expanded face-to-face time for each class period allowing for multiple activities in a single day. A typical week provides two one-hour-and-thirty-five-minute classes (Tuesday and Thursday) and one fifty-five-minute class (Friday). As with many block schedules, her students lose the continuity of everyday meetings, requiring more individual student responsibility for out-of-class work. The school also allows students to register for writing classes without regard to their grade level. Because of the cross-grade-level grouping, we know that the range of skills in the class will be disparate.

External requirements are substantial in Tracy's setting. Not only are her students subject to local and state standards, but the specter of state exit tests and college entry tests are ever present. In response to these multiple factors, the high school workshop Tracy plans represents a melding of individually selected reading and writing experiences and whole group work in nonfiction genres organized within teacher-developed thematic units. Plans, designed to honor Tracy's beliefs about best practices for teaching writing and her understanding of the importance of building community, provide diverse reading and writing opportunities with ample time for discussion to engage individual thinking and writing.

As mature writers, Tracy and I read and write in an array of genres. The more familiar the genre, the easier it is to conceptualize composing original work in that form. When we talk about ourselves as writers and what we do when we aspire to write in a less frequently used genre, we recognize familiar patterns. For example, when contemplating composing an article for a journal that perhaps speaks to principals or school board members instead of high school teachers, the pattern always tends to be the same: get back copies of the journals and read them carefully. Not only does this step help us identify the types of works a particular publication includes, it also suggests the types of genres accepted, what the audience anticipates, and even some information about word choice, sentence structure, and organization.

Because we share Tom Romano's dislike of "exposure" to literature (2000, 43), we opt for quality immersion experiences with challenging literature in the workshop, literature that addresses big ideas for each of the nonfiction genres selected for study during the semester. These readings provide the basis for whole-group experiences and conversations and allows students opportunities to "crystallize" their own sense of a work (Rosenblatt 1978, 133) and to sense the possibilities and restraints represented by the selected genre before they begin to consciously apply their knowledge of craft to their own writing.

Though interaction with literature plays a vital role in supporting young writers, it isn't enough. Critical to the success of the workshop is ample time for writers to engage in real writing—both inside and outside of class. Authors like Julia Cameron (1992, 2004) urge aspiring writers to maintain a writing journal, writing everyday, first thing in the morning, to keep the flow of words coming; she also encourages special "artist dates" each week to fuel the fire of ideas and perspectives. Because experience plays such a crucial role for writers, we agree that the use of powerful literature and a host of in-class experiences will be woven in across the semester.

Surrounding young writers with rich reading experiences provides the opportunity to help them sense the power and permanence of the written word and see how writers use language and genre in purposeful ways. We want students to understand that, for an author, *genre is a choice*. A writer selects a particular genre because it supports better than any other the message she is attempting to communicate. We believe that through genre exploration within a workshop classroom, students develop a consciousness about the rhetorical choices that writers make—an awareness that leads to recognition of their own power and responsibility as a writer and sculptor of written messages.

Our experience also tells us that it is one thing to read in a genre and quite another to write in it. To be successful writing in new genres, students require opportunities to investigate the essential qualities of the genre. They need supportive instruction to help them learn new strategies for developing ideas, organizing information, and moving from thought to paper. They need strategies to help them see their words with fresh eyes and to support revision. Further, they need other strategies to support editing and moving selected pieces to final drafts.

For these strategies—offered as skills and craft lessons—we anticipate making use of strategies available in professional literature—such as Barry Lane's (1993) "thoughtshots" (44–69) and "snapshots" (32–50)—as well as teacher-created minilessons to address issues that emerge from the students' writing. All of these strategies provide useful tools that students can draw on in the future as they apply them independently in new writing situations.

We also recognize the potential of rubrics as tools to support inquiry into genre through focused discussions about text features such as organization, word choice, sentence fluency, and voice. Lessons emerging from those discussions help students think about special features of craft and move those features into their own writing. As is suggested in a broad body of research (see Bangert-Drowns et al. 1991; Butler and Winne 1995; Strickland and Strickland 1998; and reports from Project Zero 2003), rubrics can be effective tools for supporting learning when students are encouraged to use them for feedback and self-monitoring. Our use of rubrics aims to help students develop strong mental models for continuous monitoring, revisioning, and reflecting.

Our discussions lead us to identify core components that define our vision of the high school workshop classroom. These include

- providing real time for reading, writing, and experiencing in the classroom;
- exploring new genres through rich immersion into literature;
- providing choice and encouraging student ownership in as many ways as possible;
- investigating new genres through the use of rubric-based discussions;
- providing ample scaffolding to teach new strategies for exploring and developing ideas, organizing and drafting, revising and editing;
- providing skills and craft lessons addressing student needs identified from samples of student writing, and contextualizing those skills and techniques directly in subsequent student reading and writing;
- establishing real audiences for writing including peer response, conferences with the teacher, and various modes—both written and oral—of author shares.

Tracy and I share the belief that structuring a workshop classroom reflecting these core components not only leads to a better instructional environment for students in the short term, but also helps prepare students for participation in a democratic society in significant ways as they draw on multiple perspectives, take on greater responsibility for supporting the writing of peers, and claim responsibility for their own writing voice.

In addition to student benefits, we anticipate benefits for ourselves as well. As Kathy Rowlands (1995) notes, "a student-centered workshop classroom requires meticulous procedural planning, as [students] learn how to assume their responsibilities as learners." However, the gain for both learners and teacher is substantial for "once implemented such classrooms are energizing (not exhausting) for the teacher, and typically many behavioral issues disappear, creating time for teachers to attend to the needs of students requiring additional support."

Taking a Step Back

Teaching can be a lonely enterprise. Dan Lorti (1975) described the isolation teachers experience when cut off from colleagues by the demands of the classroom and the barrier of walls. This isolation isn't limited to the K–12 environment. University teachers often find it equally challenging to find "habitable spaces" for professional conversation, sharing, and planning.

The collaboration Tracy and I develop as we work together to develop a high school workshop depends on trust established during earlier projects. That trust is essential. When courting change, we must be willing to name our beliefs, to articulate our values, and to scrutinize our plans and practices to see how well those beliefs are reflected. Trust proves a vital link that allows us to go out on a limb, think about things in new and different ways, challenge conventional wisdom about what a workshop ought to be, and ultimately, sketch out plans that represent our best judgment of successful writing environments.

Neither genre study nor workshop are new concepts. Many colleagues such as Cathy Fleischer (2005), Heather Lattimer (2003), Tom Romano (2000), Stephanie Harvey (1998), Peter Rabinowitz and Michael Smith (1998), Randy Bomer (1995), and Kathy Short and Kathryn Mitchell Pierce (1990), among others, have helped to shape our thinking about genre as a focus for reading and writing instruction. Workshop as described in ample professional literature, including books by Sheridan Blau (2003), Nancie Atwell (1998, 1987), Linda Rief (1992), Kathleen Andrasick (1990), Lucy Calkins (1983), and others, has an established model that is generally predictable in format and structure. For us, the most daunting part of the task was not understanding what others thought, but distilling the core values of genre study within a workshop for ourselves and then thinking hard about how those values might look in a high school setting. This process of distillation proved to be particularly valuable. Too often in education we toss around terms lightly, like a beach ball bouncing from hand to hand, with an assumption that all who touch it will share the same understanding of meaning and significance. Defining the features of workshop we deem essential helped us use those features as a lens for planning, leading us to ask at every juncture

- Where is the choice?
- Is there enough time for real reading and real writing?
- Are new strategies sufficiently scaffolded for students?

Those core values act as a rubric against which we can evaluate daily, weekly, and unit plans to determine how true we have been to the beliefs we profess.

The opportunity to sit together, sharing professional readings, beliefs about teaching, and questions about effective practices provides rich possibility for staying connected to other perspectives. Not only does our collaboration diminish the barrier of walls, it shrinks the distance between high school and college teaching, allowing us both to feel more authentic in our work with students.

High school is a unique setting. The local, state, and national pressures are real and affect all grade levels, but at high school the stakes are sometimes dizzying. In Michigan, for example, a major state goal is to prepare all students for college; all graduating seniors will soon take a variation of the ACT college entrance exam as their high school exit exam, and state standards themselves have recently been revised. In such circumstances, it is sometimes easy to feel lost and overwhelmed by the force of shifting demands. We find this an excellent juncture to take a deep breath, think about what we really want to accomplish with the young adults in our charge, and move ahead.

2

Establishing a Workshop Culture

Do I need to be able to write to be here?

—Thomas, ninth grade

Day One, Getting Started

On the first day of the new semester, Tracy meets Thomas and Christopher with a smile and a set of playing cards as they saunter into the classroom asking, "Is this writer's workshop?" and "Do I need to be able to write to be in here?" Earlier in the day, Tracy had arranged the twenty-eight desks in pods of four around the perimeter of the room with each desk in the pod sporting a playing card. Thomas pulls a four of diamonds from the stack, moves about the room to find his desk, and watches to see who will draw the four of hearts, spades, and clubs. These students will be his writing partners for the day.

Tracy briefly introduces herself to the diverse group of students who represent grades 9–12, and hands each student a copy of the following Writing Survey.

Writing Survey
- How do you feel about writing?
- Why do people write?
- Why do you write?
- What is the best thing that you have ever written? Why?
- What is the worst thing that you have ever written?
- How often do you write?
- What do you think a person needs to do to be a writer?

As students move quickly to address the questions, she takes care of housekeeping: attendance, scattered individual concerns, queries about names and nicknames for students she does not know. Ten minutes into the class, she interrupts the students to provide a first writing invitation so that students who finish the survey early move seamlessly into the new task.

Writing Invitation 1

Tell me a story. It can be completely true, completely made up, or somewhere in between. You decide. You can use a genre of your choice to get your words and the story on the page. This means you can tell your story using poetry, short story, essay, news article, playwriting, screenwriting, etc. Use all of the time that I give you to write. If you do any sketching or outlining, please turn it in with your writing. *Do your best.*

In case students have not acquired a writer's notebook yet, she provides lined paper at each pod of desks. The writing invitation is very open; students are asked to write in response to the prompt for ten minutes, telling any story they would like to tell and in any genre they choose. Tracy explains that this fastwrite will provide her with useful information about their rough draft writing skills.

Tracy sits at the front of the room, her head bent over her own writing. All around the room students hunch over papers, sometimes looking up for a few moments to think before beginning again. Tracy gives a two-minutes warning and encourages students to continue writing, to get down all that they can.

We are twenty minutes into a new semester. Students have completed a survey and a fastwrite, and Tracy has both taken care of class business and completed a fastwrite herself. It's time for a first experience with a writing group. Tracy recognizes the varying levels of writing confidence in the room and that many students do not know each other yet, so she encourages the students to take a few minutes to introduce themselves in their group and to share their pieces verbatim if they are willing. For students who are reluctant to read, she asks that they talk about what they have written. There's a momentary awkwardness around the room; then the talking begins.

Okay, hi. My name is Zane . . . and I wrote about a trip I took with my family . . . and . . .

On a drive home from a friend's house, sitting in the passenger seat . . . you always think you're doing fine till you get lost. Lost in everything. The roads, the music, your mind. (Abby)

Around the room students read or talk about their fastwrites: about driving to McDonald's, being in a fight, going to a family cabin every summer, taking private walks, about a mom who is a "fake liberal" but who "does not like to go against the grain" when it comes to real issues.

The reading and talking are important. Not only do these activities break the ice, they also contribute to the sense of community and audience that will be so vital to the success of the overall workshop for the semester. The sharing takes place efficiently, and soon Tracy collects the papers. At a later time, she'll analyze these along with the writing surveys; the information gained will help her plan lessons for the semester so that the instruction she provides will address the specific needs and interests demonstrated by her students.

Tracy talks the students through a tour of resources around the classroom. Resources in the room include writing materials, handbooks, a couple of computers, and lots of books. In the far back corner stands three sets of bookcases that contain a collection of literature she has assembled from yard sales, donations, and used book stores over the past eight and a half years. She explains that they will be reading a great deal in writing workshop, sometimes sharing a book as a whole class and other times using books as examples for writing techniques. Students are invited to take books out, but also to bring them back and to contribute books they no longer need from their own libraries. Tracy takes this moment as an opportunity to talk about how some books may be more appropriate for one individual than another at a particular time, and she shares a couple of examples, describing the power of several pieces of literature for her at specific points of her life.

Building community is a top priority for Tracy on this first day. Following her tour of the classroom, she invites the students to come and sit in the open space on the floor. With a few moans and groans, students move to the new area. Tracy joins the circle and, holding a ball of tightly woven string, she talks a bit about herself as a writer, about how writing has grown in importance for her as she has moved through various experiences in her life. She tosses the ball to a student who sits across the circle while continuing to hold on to a piece of the string herself.

The string becomes a metaphor for the myriad ways they will be connected to one another in the workshop. One by one, the students introduce themselves to the group and describe an experience with writing. Celly talks about writing poetry during a very emotional time in her life. Stan recalls a teacher from back in seventh grade who "really pushed me, wanted me to get something published." Victoria describes taking two classes at a local college during the summer and about being encouraged to write an essay on black rappers using vocabulary and sentence structures studied in the class. John offers up a fifth grade DARE essay that was selected for sharing, and Christopher describes writing page after page in third grade—a positive memory of writing fluency.

Many students, like Thomas who describes his ninth-grade writing as being at about a third-grade level and Barry who describes getting a poem published in a school anthology only to suffer ridicule from friends, open the window to negative feelings associated with writing. Some, like Lucas, simply have few experiences to share. Writing has not been a priority in his education to this point. Others, like Zane, recall teachers at the primary or intermediate level who encouraged writing everyday. When students arrive at the high school door, they bring with them a lengthy educational history. Often, they have developed deeply rooted attitudes about writing, and many bring with them inhibitions and fears.

As the stories are told, the ball of string is tossed from person to person, forming a physical web that becomes complex and interwoven, ultimately linking every member of the class. After the last student shares, Tracy asks the group to help her see how long it will take for a pulse to make it from her, the first person to share, to the last. The web tightens, and she gently tugs at her string. There are false starts and delays; the first attempt takes about twenty-seven seconds. They can do better, they decide. Once again, Tracy pulses her end of the string, and around the circle members wait with anticipation to receive and pass along the pulse. Fourteen seconds. A final time, everyone concentrates, and the pulse zings around the web in ten seconds!

"Why do we do this?" Tracy asks. She describes the web activity as a rich metaphor for the writing workshop. "We are all so connected in a workshop," she stresses. "When anyone comes in late or unprepared, we are all affected. When we think about writing as thinking, it's easy to see how distractions of any kind take away energy from the group." She describes ways the group can work together to keep the energy in the room and how actions can be respectful or disrespectful of other writers.

Students comment on how interesting it is to hear how far back some classmates can remember writing incidents, and how vastly different those experiences have been. The web activity provides a platform to talk briefly about the importance of trust and communication in a workshop, of how scary writing is for some classmates, and how important it will be to build an atmosphere of support for risk taking. There will be a conversation at the next class to fully acquaint students with the curricular expectations for the semester. For now, the most important issue is establishing social responsibility and collegiality.

We near the end of the class period. Students move back to their desks for a final writing invitation. Tracy moves to the overhead projector to capture brainstormed responses to this prompt.

Writing Invitation 2
What types of information would be helpful for me to know about you so that I can work effectively with you this semester?

Contributions come in quickly: my age, my name, my interests and hobbies; my attitude . . . what makes me tick; my goals . . . short term and long term and my goals for writing; my interests beyond school; facts about my family; the kinds of writing I like or don't like. Tracy adds to the list a few practical things that would help her. How are you doing in school? How should I contact your parents if the need arises? What do you need from me this semester? How can I help you grow as a writer?

Then the table is turned. "What information would be helpful for you in a letter from me?" Tracy asks. Many of the categories overlap; two are new. Students want to know about Tracy's interest in being a teacher. And, they want to know about how she will grade their writing. Soon, heads are bent toward paper as students and teacher write letters. Other than the hum of the overhead project and the scratching of pens on paper, there is silence in the room.

With ten minutes to go in the class period, Tracy interrupts the writers once again. She describes the writing homework assignment (Writing Assignment 1) due on Thursday—two days away. She explains briefly the concept of "explode a moment" and "turning the knob" (Lane 1993, 20–22, 66–75) and gives additional details about the use of the writer's notebook.

Writing Assignment 1: Writing Possibilities

   I.   In your notebook, write down the following

       10 of the best things that have ever happened to you
       10 of the worst things that have ever happened to you
       10 things that you are proud of
       10 moments with family or friends
       10 learning experiences (life or school)

  II. Take one experience from your list and write all of the details that you can remember about that moment. Write with the following senses in mind: sight, smell, taste, sound, and touch. This is called "turning the knob." You should always try to make your writing come alive so your reader feels as if they are there.

 III. Take that same experience and pinpoint an important moment. For example, it could be the moment that you slid into home plate and won the championship game. This is the big scene in your story where seconds feel like minutes or even hours. It is often a moment that is anxiously awaited or fearfully dreaded. This is called *explode a moment*. For example: Each time my foot landed a puff of dust billowed up from the ground. Tiny grains of sand were blasted with my shins as I ran full force into them. The home plate's edges were covered with dust, but its center stuck out like a flashlight in my eyes. I didn't hear the crowd cheering, and I didn't see my mom jumping up and down on the home plate fence. My muscles extended beyond their ability and each stride grew in inches. The presence of my enemy, the ball, was creeping up behind me.

I knew that it was time to slide along the dry sand. I dove down with my right arm flying through the air like Superman's always did. I squinted my eyes and looked through the dust. I couldn't help inhaling particles of dirt that clung to the inside of my nose. As I heard the ball break the air above me, I felt my hand extend further. It smacked home plate with a heaviness so complete that the sound could have been mistaken for being a hundred-pound weight. As my hand rested on the plate and my chest heaved up and down gasping for air, I heard the ball smacking into the catcher's glove just a second too late.

IV. Use turning the knob and explode a moment to tell part of a story. Please type your work. Pay close attention to sensory detail as you write.

Skills and craft lessons go in the back of the notebook, starting on the back page and working toward the front. Writing invitations of all sorts will go in the notebook as well, starting at the front of the notebook and working toward the back. Tracy agrees that any writing can be composed at the keyboard and moved to the notebook as needed. She directs attention to a sentence construction in the assignment sheet—the second sentence in section II where she has deliberately revised a sentence to include a colon—and elaborates on the way they will be experimenting with punctuation and sentence structure as an ongoing part of their work throughout the semester. She shares the first skills notes for the semester and instructs students to add these notes to the skills section of their writer's notebook.

Skills Notes 1: Colon
A colon is used to introduce a list.
Example: I love all kinds of chocolate: peanut butter cups, truffles,
M&Ms, and hot fudge.

Skills Notes 2: Semicolon
A semicolon is used to join two or more independent clauses that are not
connected with a coordinating conjunction. In other words, each of the
clauses could stand alone as a separate sentence.
Example: I had never gone to a school dance before; I was the one hovering
in the corner watching every one else have fun.

With a quick reminder of her planning time hours and the times she can be reached before or after school, the class is complete.

Plans for Day One	
Time	**Tasks**
12:05–12:25	Hand out cards for heterogeneous grouping. Complete writing survey. Post writing invitation up on the board for students to begin as soon as surveys are complete.
12:25–12:40	Small group conversations: introductions and sharing of the fastwrites—either verbatim or talking about the writing.
12:40–1:10	Whole group, string toss activity.
1:10–1:30	Letter writing activity: brainstorm information to include. Writing time.
1:30–1:40	Wrap up and homework description.

Day Two, Settling In

Tracy once again meets her students at the door, cards in hand. She'll repeat this process each day until she's sure students know one another and have developed a sense of community in the classroom. As the students settle in, they discover a photograph on the overhead projector of a boy jumping into the water. Tracy directs them to write from the boy's perspective, using the concept of explode a moment they had practiced for homework. She realizes that some of her students are very reluctant about writing, so she also provides a prompt in case anyone needs it.

I had never jumped in the water before; I was always the one slumped on the grass watching the others . . .

As heads are bent over the writing, Tracy moves softly around the room, placing cups of M&Ms at each pod of desks. Each student picks up a few, but before the candy can be popped into mouths Tracy invites students to introduce themselves to their new partners and to say one interesting thing about themselves for each piece of candy they took. Despite good-natured groans around the room, group members quickly move into a hum of conversation.

Moments later, Tracy interrupts again, asking students to share their lists from their first writing assignment and to read their explode-a-moment fastwrites to their group members. Unlike yesterday, this time she asks them to read verbatim from their papers and to select one from the group for sharing with the whole class. If a student is too nervous to read, he may allow another student to read the piece for him. Most groups move seamlessly into the reading and soon after into sharing selected pieces for the entire class to enjoy. Lily shares her writing possibilities (see Figure 2.1).

Tracy draws the group back for a quick lesson on supportive ways to provide feedback, encouraging students to think about the papers they have just heard and select lines they recall to be powerful, thought provoking, or unique. Later she will review the papers to scout for writing strengths and patterns of errors; these will support her decisions about future minilessons. For now, a chorus of lines chimes out . . .

> "I crashed in the water with the force of a wrecking ball."
> "I felt as if I were a baby bird on a flag pole on the thirty-first floor."
> "Gravity would have no problem with me today."
> "The water rippled and coiled under me."
> "I could smell the lake."
> "The yell rippled the water."
> "Like the little mermaid, I wanted to know what the other people knew. Yet, I knew that water and black people just don't mix."
> "The air lifted a one-hundred-pound weight off my chest."
> "I gasped for air and a giant gnat flew in."

. . . and cool phrases filled the air as Tracy races to capture them on an overhead transparency.

> ". . . cool green grass . . . hot board"
> ". . . magical moment . . . "
> ". . . silent liquid . . . "
> ". . . free and flying . . . "
> ". . . reflection of trees on the water."

Tracy describes why they are taking the time to think about interesting, descriptive lines, and explains that throughout the semester they will pause often in the midst of reading and writing to think together about author's craft so that they will be able to use similar techniques in their own writing.

This is the moment that Tracy chooses to provide students with a syllabus and list of expectations for the semester (see Appendix C). Written in the genre of a

I. In your notebook, write down the following

Best Things

getting into Community
moving to Ann Arbor
being in Burns Park and Tappan Players
participating in the Pioneer Swim Team
going to camp
getting confirmed
becoming friends with Maya

Worst Things

parents getting a divorce
having asthma attacks
joining synchronized swimming
Grandpa dying
cutting my eye
finding out my dad smokes
leaving Chicago
getting a babysitting job

Proud of

my grades
my attitude
my friends
my family
my goals
my opinions
my room
my swim team
my muscles

Moments with My Family/Friends

Christmas at Nebraska
Christmas in Philadelphia—burp guns
homecoming
playing pick-up sticks
Minnesota—hurt my neck
horseback riding
jump roping
hip hop class

Figure 2.1. Lily's Writing Possibilities/Explode a Moment

Learning Experiences

pushing Andy down a muddy hill
kicking rafe
stealing cookies
watching scary movie
joining Hamlet
joining PHS swim team
going to camp
tasting wine for the first time
yelling at my mom
trying to hit my older brother

II. Take one experience from your list and write all of the details that you can remember about that moment.

stands—wave of purple
heart and stomach clenching
the blocks were full
chlorine-smell filled my lungs
taste, 2 Reese's ate earlier
people talking
gun going off
diving off in slow-motion
feeling the water pour over me
my lungs tightening
heart racing
flip turn—can't breathe, can't breathe!
head spinning
sense of dread—75 to go!
pulled myself out—hacking and crying
locker room . . . so scared
collapse on floor of locker room under the showers
so afraid . . . so afraid of the water
inhaler—breathing in and out—miracle drug

III. Explode a Moment

It was my turn.
"200 individual medley, heat one" The voice of the announcer rang through the pool like the bells of the dead.
My stomach churned. I looked into the stands, a sea of purple, my mother's cheery, confident face. What the hell do I think I am doing?

Figure 2.1. *Continued*

Gunfire.

My body flows perfectly into the water. Coming out of my streamline I reach above my head and push my body forward. Again and again I reach for the wall. But as I count the number of laps it only seems to take longer.

My lungs tighten, and still I push onward. Plunging my face into the water, as my hands pull forward.

I try so hard, but still, three laps to go. I can't, can't. I am going to die. I can't swim any further.

Pulling myself out of the water with the speed and strength of experience, I crash to the ground, hacking and breathing rapidly.

So much noise!

My mother's firm grip pulls me to my feet and we hurry to the locker room. Friends touch me lightly on the shoulder like angels. We reach the locker room.

I scream in terror and disbelief.

Collapsing on the ground under the showers, I cry and shake.

So afraid.

I clutch the small tube and inhale as though it were a miracle drug.

My breathing relaxes! I sob and shake in my mother's arms: this was not the first time my lungs have stolen my air.

Figure 2.1. *Continued*

letter, the syllabus highlights the components Tracy feels essential to the success of their workshop: time, ownership, response, and community. Though she has included written details about expectations, she reviews several with the group as a whole, reminding students of the web of string from the previous class and the metaphor it represents, of how every single action in the classroom affects everyone in the workshop just the way a single pulse could affect everyone on the web. Tracy wants her students to keep in mind that writing involves risk taking, and that risk taking requires safety that only a community can provide.

With a quick transition, a large cluster of pictures taken from magazines is spread across the floor, and students move forward to select one. Tracy invites them to jot down a list of details they see in their picture, and I join in.

I have a woman . . . older. She's wearing a crown and there's a bottle of champagne with a cake . . . maybe angel food? There's the number sixteen on top of the cake.

Through three fastwrites, students practice moving from being on the inside with first-person point of view,

> I've never seen Granny more radiant. Who would know that she needs oxygen almost all the time. On this special night—her ninetieth birthday—she's conditioned herself not to need it, at least for a few hours; not to use her walking cane; not to feel old. Her smile lights up the room and warms us all. Someone from the outside would wonder about the sixteen candles on her cake. I know it's a little bit of family humor . . . one candle for each of us sixteen grandchildren.

to the outside with third-person point of view,

> Dera Mabry, ninety years old, walked into the birthday party on her son's arm, like a princess walking proudly into the prom. She paused for moment as she surveyed the folks gathered for her special day, then broke into a smile that literally lit up the room.

and finally to third-person omniscient point of view.

> "I am so blessed," she thought. "I'm so, so blessed." Dera walked carefully, her arm supported by her son, stepping gracefully into the glowing room. "Who'd a thought I could live to see my ninetieth birthday?" she questioned to those clustered nearest her. As James moved her gently into the room, navigated her to the waiting rocking chair, the crowd of children, grand and great-grandchildren, friends, and neighbors collectively breathed a prayer of gratitude for such a joyful spirit.

Having experienced the shift in stance in the story through their writing, students are ready to receive Tracy's short minilesson on point of view. She directs them to the very back of their writer's notebook where they will again add materials from the back toward the front in the skills and craft section. Figure 2.2 reviews first-person, third-person, and third-person omniscient point of view.

Which was easiest for you?" Tracy asks, encouraging students to talk about why one point of view might be more challenging for them than another. They look together at the example excerpts. The discussion of examples provides an excellent moment to offer up new skills notes.

Skills Notes 3: Citation guide for stories, essays, books
Short stories and essays are in quotation marks and books are underlined or italicized. When using MLA format for quotations, the page number goes inside the period when the quote is four lines or less. Using p. or pg. or pp. is incorrect. When the quote is more than four lines, you use a block quote format that is double-spaced and indented. The final period goes before the parenthesis and the page number as in the following example from *The Pearl* by John Steinbeck.

First-person

In the first-person point of view, the story is told by one of the characters. For example, *Stargirl* by Jerry Spinelli is told in the first-person:

> At the time I simply considered the episode a mystery. It did not occur to me that I was being watched. We were all being watched. (2)

David Sedaris also writes using first-person in his essay "Go Carolina" from *Me Talk Pretty One Day*:

> The agent came for me during geography lesson. She entered the room and nodded at my fifth-grade teacher, who stood frowning at the map of Europe. What would needle me later was the realization that this had all been prearranged. My capture had been scheduled to go down at exactly 2:30 on a Thursday afternoon. (4)

Third-person

Third-person point of view is when you tell the story from the point of view of someone who is outside it. John Steinbeck uses third-person point of view in his novel *The Pearl*:

> Kino awakened in the near dark. The stars still shone and the day had drawn only a pale wash of light in the lower sky to the east. The roosters had been crowing for some time, and the early pigs were already beginning their ceaseless turning of twigs and bits of wood to see whether anything to eat had been overlooked. (1)

Third-person omniscient (all knowing)

Third-person omniscient point of view is when the story is written from an outside source who knows what everyone is thinking and feeling. When you use third-person omniscient, you can reveal the innermost feelings and thoughts of multiple characters as with Kira in Lois Lowry's *Gathering Blue*.

> The chief guardian stood. "Do you wish to speak?" he asked Kira for the third time. For the third time she shook her head no. She felt terribly tired. (37)

Figure 2.2. Craft Lesson: Point of View

> Kino awakened in the near dark. The stars still shone and the day had drawn only a pale wash of light in the lower sky to the east. The roosters had been crowing for some time, and the early pigs were already beginning their ceaseless turning of twigs and bits of wood to see whether anything to eat had been overlooked. (1)

As with all skills and craft notes, these will be referred to and built on numerous times during the semester, often in very short microlessons that may be shared in whole group, in peer writing groups, or during individual conferences.

With class rapidly drawing to a close, students once again take out their homework from the previous class. Looking over the fastwrites, the groups of four review one another's papers, responding to two prompts.

1. Select specific lines and/or words you like.
2. Respond to the content of the piece by thinking about personal connections.

Elizabeth chose to write about a day at the beach. In her excerpt, lines selected by her response group are italicized.

> The *water tasted salty and thick*. When I would look at the sun my eyes would sting because of the salt. The boogie board that I was on had left marks on my stomach that also constantly stung because of the salty water. *Catching the perfect wave was like winning the lottery for me.* The white foam was just above my head, following me into the beach as if to catch up with me but never could. *The powerful water sounded like base drums crashing in the basement.*

Her response partners wrote

1. I have only been to the ocean once that I can remember. Your piece totally brought me back to it.
2. I remember swallowing a mouthful of ocean water the first time I went to the beach. That first line brought that memory back.
3. Nice beginning. The first paragraph reminded me of the pain of defeat.

Students eagerly receive their papers back, scan comments with smiles, then surrender papers and responses to Tracy for her responses. With one minute to go before students dash to their next classes Tracy asks, "What are your writing goals for the semester? Think about this and jot them down before our next class."

Taking a Step Back

From the first moment of class, Tracy places great value on developing a community of writers. With the help of two packs of playing cards, she seats students

Plans for Day Two	
Time	**Tasks**
12:05–12:30	Hand out cards for heterogeneous grouping. Complete fastwrite from photo. Small group introductions and sharing of fastwrites.
12:30–12:55	Whole group sharing of selected fastwrites. Sharing of cool phrases and sentences. Short minilesson on the significance of word choice.
12:55–1:00	Review of syllabus and expectations.
1:00–1:30	Fastwrites on point of view.
1:30–1:40	Peer feedback on explode-a-moment and snapshots papers.

randomly in the classroom. This accomplishes several things. First, it helps to break down cliques of students who might otherwise have clustered together by age, culture, or gender. By establishing heterogeneous groups and providing several nonthreatening opportunities for sharing, she supports the establishment of new, small, safe communities within the classroom. Building on this, the whole group sharing with the aid of the web of string helps to extend the sense that the class itself will be a community—a place where everyone is safe, where taking risks is okay, and where everyone has a responsibility to support the growth of everyone else.

When the National Writing Project (NWP) was established in 1974, founder James Gray argued that the knowledge needed to improve writing in the nation's schools already existed in the best practices of excellent teachers (Blau 2003, 14). NWP teachers hold dear the precepts that teachers of writing must be writers themselves and that as consultants they would only model practices they engage in themselves. As a teacher consultant with the Eastern Michigan Writing Project (EMWP), Tracy reflects her work with the project in a variety of ways in her classroom.

Tracy demonstrates a strong belief that writing teachers must be writers themselves. At each juncture of the first day of writer's workshop, she writes with her students. The result is powerful modeling. She assumes that her students will learn to write by engaging in writing. From the initial Writing Survey, to the first fastwrite, to the letter written with a clear audience and purpose, students learn that this class will be one in which writing is center stage, not just a skill to be studied or discussed. Here, writing isn't an afterthought, it's the main event!

During the first day of writing workshop, Tracy learns a great deal from and about her students. A quick sort of the writing surveys reveals that seven of the students do not write at all and another seven write only for school assignments. Of the remaining half of the class, students often wait for inspiration to write and demonstrate little knowledge of the processes writers use. Moreover, student genres of choice generally reflect expressive writing (Britton et al. 1975, 126–127), including diaries, journals, or notes written for personal purposes. Only two of the students mention writing poetry and none mention other creative genres. Overwhelmingly, students cite school essays—particularly five-paragraph essays—as the worst writing they have done. These findings suggest a strong need to build confidence and interest and to broaden the scope of genres for which the young adult authors feel a degree of comfort.

From the Writing Survey Tracy also learns specific information about individual students. For example, she finds that Lucas feels reluctance about writing and has substantial gaps in his writing background; she learns that he has difficulty remembering ideas for writing and staying focused on an idea when he has a good one; she discovers that he has struggled with dyslexia, which he feels has negatively impacted his reading and writing. She discovers that while Celly currently avoids writing in and out of school, as a young writer she maintained diaries over a period of years. She notes that Abby and Elizabeth both enjoy writing poetry. From each of her self-identified writers, she detects an understanding that a real audience is helpful.

The fastwrites and letter provide additional sources of information and represent a type of ongoing assessment that Tracy will draw on as she makes instructional decisions throughout the semester. A fast analysis of the papers reveals a huge spread in skills and interests. An analysis of strengths and needs of several students will illustrate the data gathered.

Lucas is a fourteen-year-old freshman who demonstrates strong voice in his writing. He puts his learning disability up front, describing his struggle with books—he has only read eight books over fifty pages in length—and his strong desire to master the conventions of writing. An error analysis of his spelling yields numerous difficulties with homophones, predictable patterns, and rule-based words, all indicating a need for instruction that will introduce a sense of logic in the language. Lucas requests that Tracy be "patient with my spelling and punctuation." His eagerness to gain control of written language suggests a high level of readiness to learn. In the two fastwrites, he has generated 326 words.

Lily is also a fourteen-year-old freshman, but her abilities with written language distinguish her as a remarkably able student. She speaks with a candid voice about her parent's divorce, about her joy at being in this particular high school, and of her desire to better her writing skills. For her, improvement will come on top of a repertoire of strong skills. Her sentence structure is varied and well executed. Her voice, organization, and fluency are strong. She identifies her own greatest need, saying "I need to write. I almost never do, and that's really important to me." In two fastwrites, Lily generates 361 words.

At sixteen Stan represents one of the most prolific writers in the class. With excellent use of language and organization, Stan is free to exercise his writer's voice. He peppers his work with descriptive details, shares his varied interests, and demonstrates the impact books have had on his development as a writer, noting specifically *Life of Pi* and *Siddhartha*. He asks Tracy to push him to do even better. In his two fastwrites he generates 503 words.

Finally, Celly, at age eighteen, represents a writer who is exceptionally competent already. Her writer's voice is crisp and clear. Her writing reflects a smooth flow of ideas executed with skill and precision. Celly has confidence in her abilities, and from Tracy she needs "support and honest criticism." Still, she expresses strong reservations about sharing her work with others despite the fact that she holds as a goal the development of the ability to "write poems that reach out to other people." For her choice of genre in one fastwrite, she chose an obituary and her narrative suggests a strong interest in exploring other genres that may be new to her. Her two fastwrites have generated 341 words.

Each piece of student writing will be stored in the writer's notebook or in a working portfolio that students will add to throughout the semester. For now, there are immediate benefits for Tracy and her students. Within the community being developed, students recognize that their teacher strives to know them and their needs personally. And, students have already begun the important task of becoming reflective about their work and their goals. There is no mistaking the fact that in this class, the reading and writing are the focus of the curriculum.

From the first few moments of the second class, it is evident that students have already accepted the expectation of writing and sharing as the normal daily practice of the workshop classroom. Each student comes in, takes her card, finds her new seat, and begins with the business of the day. Already, Tracy and her students appear to have bonded into a supportive community. As a guest in the room, I am surprised with three things: how little time is wasted in transition to class and to various activities during class; how all students begin writing without question; and how smoothly peer sharing emerges. I've been a teacher for a long time, and I know these features never "just happen."

Day two continues to be a time of sculpting a "habitable space" (Fleischer and Schaafsma 1998, vii–xxxii) where writers and readers feel safe to take chances, to give and receive constructive response. More than just basic reading and writing skills is core here. There is a vision that literacy is complex, multifaceted, and powerful. The valuing of the individual and her stories moves the classroom "toward a multi-voiced literacy in which all might speak, no matter what language, to reach toward responsive understanding of deeper meanings of language and of the word as they shape worlds [they] must inhabit" (Robinson 1998, 285).

During the initial fastwrite and sharing, students experience a carefully scaffolded process that supports insecure writers and allows safety nets in groups as they share for the first time with new response partners. Rosenblatt reminds us that "language is at once basically social and intensely individual" (1978, 20). Tracy encourages students to value their own thoughts and trust themselves as writers. She encourages them also to remember that the story or the poem may represent a different experience to different readers. By establishing an environment of sharing, response allows the novice writer to gain multiple perspectives on something as basic as what her story is all about. And, these perspectives, when reflected back to the writer, allow the opportunity to think about one's work with new eyes—even before conversations about revision have taken place.

Today, both skills and craft lessons weave seamlessly into the class. From the sharing of selected fastwrites, the class turns its attention to the beauty of rich language. Verbal sharing, capturing effective words and sentences on an overhead transparency, and discussing why some words and phrases are more memorable than others, helps students to train their ears as well as their eyes to powerful language, a process that will be built on steadily across the semester. Storing such powerful vocabulary in student notebooks or on word wall posters allows ready access to them during future writing times. Beginning to think about the sound of words in beautifully crafted phrases encourages young writers to write like a reader with ears alert to the way a newly crafted written passage sounds. It also reinforces the notion that these beautiful words and sentences come from them—not a distant published author—and that they, too, are capable of creating texts that encourage others to stop and take note.

Experiencing the shifting stance of the narrator through their own writing, as in the second writing invitation during the class, clears the way for a meaningful minilesson on point of view. Students have moved beyond abstract-sounding terms; they have now felt for themselves the ways in which the story changes when inside or outside the action. Notes from the lesson are available in the students' notebooks and will be referenced frequently in coming days, allowing them to create a meaningful context for information that could otherwise feel abstract or irrelevant.

Moreover, the careful weaving of skills lessons at timely moments and the reinforcement of them in future classes increases the likelihood that they'll be remembered. As a contrast, the lesson brought forward a painful first-year teacher memory of my own when I spent a full week teaching the uses of the comma. The students learned a very important thing from the intensive week of exercises . . . the teacher likes commas. They proceeded to use them as if from a salt shaker for the rest of the term. Abundant professional literature supports the fact that skills taught in isolation tend to be forgotten quickly. Contextualizing skills within writing encourages young writers to think of skills like punctuation and capitalization as writing tools that have value.

As the teacher and students listened carefully to one another, stopping for clarification and for comments, another significant thing happened: more students began to demonstrate investment in the texts they had written. This, too, illuminated the necessity of having something to say . . . something the writer is concerned about or interested in . . . before issues of grammar or spelling or punctuation will matter.

The syllabus for the workshop spelled out an array of high expectations that meet or exceed state standards. Richard Allington, president of the International Reading Association, laments the lack of a sense of urgency in many academic settings where children struggle with learning to read. He stresses "to achieve the highest quality of education outcomes, that we make every moment of the school day count" (2005, 17). Time is used efficiently in the writing workshop; the structure of the workshop itself has been quickly established and now contributes to the smooth running of the classroom. While the authors of *The Neglected R* lament the fact that most high school students will write less than a few pages a semester, the workshop students understand that they will produce ten to fifteen pages a week. Granted, this includes drafts and revisions. Nonetheless, the production of so many pages of writing— with continuous opportunities to receive input and to use the responses for refinement of selected pieces—provides an amazing platform for growth. With the community established and functioning, Tracy and her students look toward moving into a thematic unit focused on nonfiction writing.

Part 2

• • • • • •

Thematic Focus on Nonfiction

This semester Tracy's class will study nonfiction genres through a variety of multiweek units. The first unit, offered here in detail, explores the way an author's purpose frames choice of a particular genre and how that choice supports a message. In this unit, students have opportunities to choose topics for both the short in-class and longer outside-of-class pieces. In addition, students are allowed to select the most appropriate nonfiction genre for their final piece of writing, which will culminate the unit.

Generally genre and thematic studies are looked on as two separate organizing structures. As Tracy developed this unit, however, her intent was to meld genre and thematic planning to demonstrate the ways various nonfiction genres provide different opportunities to relate a narrative. The class researches events that have personal significance and writes about these events in a nonfiction genre of choice.

Tracy has chosen one longer piece of literature for whole-class study—*Night*, the powerful Holocaust memoir by Elie Wiesel. This account of an actual horrific event provides a common experience for the students to read and discuss. In addition, thematically linked works of poetry, song lyrics, newspaper articles, speeches, journals and more, allow students to build a deeply textured understanding of the historical events and a sense of how one might layer the telling. By drawing on more than one genre, while focusing instruction on one in particular, students gain a deeper understanding of the events, times, and circumstances, while noticing that the lines separating genres sometimes blur. They also see how genre selection is a choice made in keeping with the author's purpose and audience.

Building upon class activities in this unit, students will take a piece of modern history and put an individual face on it, interviewing a participant whenever possible as they craft their own autobiographical or biographical account. In a subsequent thematic unit, students will take a close look at memoir. Again, rich literature will provide a backdrop for significant writing and reading from self-selected genres both in class and at home. These choice pieces of writing will provide an authentic context for ongoing skills and craft lessons.

3

Crafting Texts That Are True

Day One, Nonfiction Unit

Students gather in new writing workshop groups for the third meeting of the semester, a class separated from the first two classes by several days due to block scheduling at Tracy's school. The first week's two meetings were filled with community, fluency, and confidence building. This week, Tracy will use this new sense of community to advance students into reading and writing nonfiction.

As students settle into desks with cards in hand, opening notebooks and preparing to write, Tracy shares an overhead transparency of the poem "The Butterfly" from *I Never Saw Another Butterfly*, a heart-rending collection of poetry from children of the Holocaust.

> **The Butterfly**
> The last, the very last,
> So richly, brightly dazzlingly yellow.
> Perhaps if the sun's tears would sing
>   against a white stone . . .
>
> Such, such a yellow
> Is carried lightly 'way up high.
> It went away I'm sure because it wished to
>   kiss the world good-bye.
>
> For seven weeks I've lived in here,
> Penned up inside this ghetto.
> But I have found what I love here.
> The dandelions call to me
> And the white chestnut branches in the court.
> Only I never saw another butterfly.

That butterfly was the last one
Butterflies don't live in here,
   in the ghetto.
  —Pavel Friedmann (4.6.1943, 39)

With little discussion of the poem, Tracy asks students to open their notebooks to the skills section and take a few minutes to brainstorm ways to respond to a piece of literature. Soon, Tracy rapidly makes a list at the overhead as each student contributes a possible response.

Possibilities for Response

- Write a poem or something creative.
- Make a list of details that come to mind.
- Laugh, cry, or dance.
- Write a narrative or emotional response.
- Create a story of your own that connects.
- Write a poem on the same topic.
- Write *whatever* on how it pertains to your life.
- Make connections to other things you have read.
- Make connections to things that have happened to you or someone you know.
- Make connections to things happening in the world right now.
- Develop questions.
- Make another poem from words in the original one.
- Draw a picture or create some other type of art.
- Write and/or perform a reaction (drama).
- Create a song and/or perform it.

Students add new possibilities to their individual lists. Tracy rereads "The Butterfly" and reads for the first time "Terezin," from the same collection.

Terezin

The heaviest wheel rolls across our foreheads
To bury itself deep somewhere inside our memories.

We've suffered here more than enough,
Here in this clot of grief and shame,
Wanting a badge of blindness
To be a proof for their own children.

A fourth year of waiting, like standing above a swamp
From which any moment might gush forth a spring.
Meanwhile, the rivers flow another way,
Another way,
Not letting you die, not letting you live.

And the cannons don't scream and the guns don't bark
And you don't see blood here.
Nothing, only silent hunger.
Children steal the bread here and ask and ask
   and ask.
And all would wish to sleep, keep silent, and
    Just to go to sleep again . . .
The heaviest wheel rolls across our foreheads
To bury itself deep somewhere inside our memories.

               — Mif (1944, 17)

It is important that the students hear the power of the words of the poems. It is equally important that they read the words themselves. Tracy asks that they do so and then to respond to the invitation:

Writing Invitation 3

Create a response to either poem or to the combination of the two. Use any of the response possibilities we have generated, or if you choose, create a new one and use that.

As with most responses, the time allotted for Writing Invitation 3 is short—a mere three to five minutes. The varied responses are shared quickly around the room: Abby explores the words "the heaviest wheel" and the line "not letting you die, not letting you live." She opens up a discussion for the class about the stark imagery in the poems, the sadness and the sense of despair. Celly draws a picture, pencil lines against white paper reflecting the same starkness identified in Abby's words. Others offer up the beginnings of a song lyric, a connection to a personal feeling, a series of questions.

In their new groups, students are asked to introduce themselves and share one thing that happened over the weekend—an action that acknowledges the need for social sharing and simultaneously gets it out of the way—before creating a communal list of facts they know about the Holocaust, an exercise that draws from and builds on their prior knowledge. Soon, Tracy quickly records their facts on a transparency:

What We Know About the Holocaust

- Jews had to wear the Star of David.
- Bodies were incinerated.
- There was mass genocide of people who were not Aryans.
- gas chambers—showers
- Auschwitz was the largest concentration camp.
- Polish, gypsies, and gays also suffered discrimination.
- ghettos prior to concentration camps

- mass graves
- pogroms
- Hitler was Austrian.
- Nazis
- Medical experiments were conducted on people in the camps.
- six million killed
- Those in the camps had numbers tattooed on their skin.
- Any who opposed the Nazis were also subject to discrimination.

The community list grows, making a wealth of information visible to all.

"*Night*," Tracy tells the students, "is my favorite book to read aloud. Its message is not only intense as a story, but it is also an example of powerful writing. As she begins to read, words flow over the class; students relax, swept along with the story. Tracy stops, rereads a series of sentences.

> Then he understood. He got out of bed and with automatic movements began to get dressed. Then he went up to the bed where his wife slept and touched her brow with infinite tenderness; she opened her eyes, and it seemed to me that her lips were brushed by a smile. (13)

She asks students to look at the series of sentences: first three words in a simple sentence; then thirteen words in another simple sentence; finally a much longer compound sentence of thirty-five words made up of two sentences, themselves constructed of compound sentences. Students observe how the writer's craft draws the reader in, how varied sentence structure can open up a scene such as this one and place the reader right in the room with the characters.

Students begin reading silently for ten minutes. Toward the end of that quick timed reading, Tracy moves around the room, noting the page number each student is on. The goal is to complete the novel within a week, so it will be important for students to think about their reading speed and allot sufficient outside reading time each day to finish on schedule. By their next class on Thursday (meeting four), they are to be to page forty-five, and should record two sets of lines that they particularly like. Tracy reminds them of a previous minilesson on MLA citations, and asks them to review and then observe the correct way to cite a passage.

As the class draws to a close, she reviews once again the characteristics of nonfiction literature, explaining that *Night* is Elie Wiesel's attempt to recount an important story as accurately as he possibly can. For their own writing, it will be important to think about an important event they can share through a personal story. For their next class, students are asked to complete the following assignment:

Writing Assignment 2: Historical Events
Please write down twenty historical events that have happened since 1930. You may use resources to help you complete this.

The lists will help students begin to focus on an event for their own nonfiction story, one for which they will be able to gather information through interviews and exploration of secondary sources.

Plans for Day One, Nonfiction Unit (day three of the semester)	
Time	**Tasks**
12:05–12:20	Hand out cards for heterogeneous grouping. Sharing of "The Butterfly." Brainstorm ways of responding and add list to notebook.
12:20–12:30	Read "The Butterfly" again and "Terezin." Writing Invitation 3—Respond to one or both pieces using one of the possibilities generated or a new one of choice. Share responses
12:30–12:45	Brainstorm what we know about the Holocaust.
12:45–1:20	Tracy reads aloud from *Night.* Students discuss effective sentence structure from examples in *Night.*
1:20–1:30	Timed silent reading from *Night.*
1:30–1:40	Review of nonfiction. Homework: list of historical events and two citations of favorite passages.

Day Two, Nonfiction Unit

As students enter and find their new groups, Tracy uses overhead transparencies to display a series of newspaper articles from 1937—March 10, May 20, and July 26—tracing the progression of laws in Germany enforcing a ban on Jewish merchants and attempting to purify the Aryan race. After she reads the newspaper articles, the students volunteer responses. The articles are followed by two very different poems, one from Reverend Martin Niemöller and the other from contemporary poet Sara Holbrook.

First They Came for the Jews

First they came for the Jews
    And I did not speak out—
    Because I was not a Jew.
Then they came for the communists
    And I did not speak out—
    Because I was not a communist.
Then they came for the trade unionists
    And I did not speak out—
    Because I was not a trade unionist.
      Then they came for me—
And there was no-one left
    To speak out for me.
           —Martin Niemöller, 1938

Naked

The first time I saw a man naked,
It was not my brother.
I was born without a brother,
which everyone knows
is like being born without green hair,
or a wart on the tip of your nose.
or the skin of a reptile.

Being born with no brother was a definite asset,
or so I thought until fifth grade, when I started to wonder.
I wondered why every time I would mention the word "it,"
in any context, the boys would laugh—they'd fall on the ground.
It was as if we were tuned in to two different programs,
like they were tuned into cartoons
and I was watching a mystery.
I wondered.
And I wondered with the sense of urgency
of 4:30 in the afternoon and Mom says,
"No more snacks before dinner,"
and you're starving.
I wanted what I wanted and I wanted it now.

Prevailing neighborhood trade policies
provided for such things,
a look for a look, even up.

Worth considering,
until a permission slip came home from school.
There was to be a film about growing up.
Well, even I knew that was fiftiespeak for "naked."
My wonder swelled within me—
I had swallowed a balloon.
I couldn't breathe.
Breathless, until the film showed us diagrams.
Diagrams? Bones without the meat.
It looked like a direction sheet on how to assemble a bicycle,
absolutely no help at all. I deflated gradually.
A couple weeks later, another film.
No permission slips this time.
Just a film about the war of our fathers, World War II.
Germany. Hitler youth. Wind up soldiers.
Waving train cars.
   Pits of white, white limbs. Ovens, not for cakes.
     Three men standing against a fence, heads shaved.
      Their collar bones poking out like
        coat hangers without the clothes.
          The picture cut off at the hollow places where
           Their bellies belonged.
        Except for one man, standing in the background,
          Who stepped deliberately to the side.
        Stripped of any sense of wonder or urgency,
          he made no attempt to cover himself
        He faced the camera because he wanted me to see.

        I dragged my feet a little on the way
          Home from school that day,
       kicking aimlessly at the fallen leaves.
        Not so much in a hurry.
         After all, I had seen.
          For the first time,
          I had seen a man,
           naked.

          —Sara Holbrook (1998, 6–7)

Each poem is read through multiple times, and students are given five minutes to write in response to either the newspaper articles, one of the poems, or a combination of these artifacts. Students quickly turn to the writing in their notebooks, anticipating the opportunity to introduce themselves to their new partners and share their fastwrites.

Niemöller's poem highlights for many the horror that can come from silence and evokes questions about the world today: where is our silence or complacency resulting in horror or loss? Holbrook's poem initiates a different type of response as students connect it with their own memories. Many recall similar questions about the human body and their curiosity as younger students. Some note how sad it is that the first view of the male body the young girl experiences is that of the emaciated figure in the concentration camp. They also note how moving that experience must have been. In their small groups, Tracy asks students to consider a dilemma.

> Consider the possibility of a fire in your home. Assuming that you have been able to get all your family and pets out safely and that you have time to go back in and rescue one personal item, what would that be?

Conversation erupts around the room. While everyone can identify with the situation and most can quickly think of a special artifact to save, it takes only a few moments for students to begin problematizing the scenario. Just one item? Suddenly the dilemma becomes more complex. Does one choose something of family significance to preserve the family's history, or should the decision be based on what the family will most need in order to survive? Can one afford to be selfish at such a time and carry away a personal item for pleasure, or must one think of the needs of the group? Connection to the dilemmas faced by the displaced citizens of Europe during the Holocaust—and to displaced refugees today—come quickly.

For this class Tracy has a surprise for students: a short performance quiz on their reading of the first forty-five pages of *Night* (see Figure 3.1). Tracy's questions emphasize a number of things. First, she is interested in assuring that students are on track with their reading and assignments. Second, she reinforces the use of MLA requirements for citations, a skill she has taught and for which students have resources in their notebooks. Finally, she encourages students to develop a sense of context for their reading through connecting the events, problems, and emotions represented by the selected quotes to their own lives, the world, or the book as a whole. These are far from literal recall questions, requiring instead the ability to think critically.

The quiz serves one more purpose. Before the papers come in for assessment, Tracy asks students to read aloud the quote to which they were responding. One after the other, around the room quotes are read, some being repeated several times. Everyone contributes. Like a motion poem, one that evolves from spontaneous reading of important words or phrases from a text, the passages emphasize significant parts of the reading, bringing the book to life and initiating a conversation about why some passages might have been repeatedly selected and why those words appeal to so many readers.

I. Write a summary (between one-half and 1 page) of the events from the reading up to page 45. What happened?

II. Pick one quote from the reading and respond to it. Remember to use MLA format when you write the quote. You need to use the correct format. Create your own writing prompt for the quote or write from one of these:

- What does the quote mean in the context of the rest of the book?
- What connections can you make between the quote and the rest of the text?
- What connections can you make between the quote and other texts (poems, stories, movies, songs, etc.)?
- What connections can you make between the quote and yourself?
- What connections can you make between the quote and events in the world?
- What questions arise from the quote?
- What did the quote help you to better understand?

Figure 3.1. Quiz for *Night*, Pages 1–45

From her analysis of the students' early fastwrites Tracy has identified two areas for additional work and instructional focus: use of powerful vocabulary and appropriate paragraphing. Instead of providing lists of words for students to learn, she invites the growth of vocabulary through the development of language awareness in the materials they read and the conversations they hear. She provides a sheet for listing words of their choice—words that they notice in their reading—and a series of strategies for identifying those words (see Figure 3.2). She encourages students to pay attention to words and to deliberately use these new words that they identify to add power and spice to their writing. In short, she asks students to take ownership for their use of language.

Tracy also shares the following information on a transparency for students to copy into the skills and craft section of their notebook.

Skills Notes 4: Paragraphs
Two reasons for starting new paragraphs:

1. New topic or new idea
2. New speaker when there is a dialogue between two or more people

During the semester you will be responsible for collecting, researching, and using power words. I want you to search for words that you want to use in your own writing. Power words earn their name because they are both powerful words and they give us power to accurately and exquisitely express ourselves. Words are power.

Add words from your reading and listening to your list of power words. Write as small as you can, so you can pack the page with words! You will paperclip the power words page into your notebook. When you write, you should take this list out of your notebook, set it beside you, and try to integrate the words into the literature that you are creating.

You have three options for how to add words to your list:

1. Keep your pen in hand and your notebook close as you read; write words down as you go. (This may be distracting for some.)
2. As you are reading, keep a pen/pencil in hand and put a small dot near the word that you want to add to your list. This will help you return to the word later.
3. Look through your reading after you finish and search for the power words.

Use the option that works for you.

Figure 3.2. Power Words

The need for greater awareness of paragraphing can be traced to the students' explode-a-moment papers and she reminds them that the workshop is designed to help them grow as writers. She encourages students, "Study Wiesel's writing as we read today. Look at how and when he creates new paragraphs. I want you to read as a writer."

Students are eager to move back into their reading and welcome the opportunity to hear more of the text read aloud. Tracy takes the lead, setting up a "jump-in reading strategy" to invite multiple voices. She reads several pages of the text and then pauses, waiting for a new voice to "jump in." They do, and student after student reads until they feel ready to stop, allowing another reader to pick up the story. No one is pressured to read aloud because the text is unrehearsed and for some unrehearsed reading would present difficulty.

As the class draws to a close, students suspend reading and bring out the Events Since 1930 lists that they have generated, events varying in both their significance and range.

Events Since 1930

- *Brown v. Board of Education*, 1954
- Rwanda genocide, 1994
- Kennedy assassination, 1963
- Fourteenth Amendment
- man on the moon, 1969
- invention of Silly Putty and the Pet Rock
- invention of Wonder Bread
- September 11
- Pearl Harbor
- Rodney King riots
- Dutch Labor Party formation
- fall of the Berlin Wall
- development of oral contraceptive pills, 1961
- the Beatles
- Little Rock school desegregation
- Woodstock
- and more . . .

Tracy lays the groundwork for the nonfiction writing to come when students will select one event to focus on for research and writing. To tell the story of their selected event, by sharing the event through the eyes of a participant, much as Elie Wiesel has done in *Night*, students will need to interview a participant and complete both primary and secondary research. They are encouraged to think carefully about their choice of event before the next class and to complete the following Initial Information Sheet.

Writing Assignment 3: Nonfiction Writing Initial Information Sheet
Complete the following information as best you can. Your topic may change, but I want to see where your thoughts are right now.

1. What historical event do you want to focus on?
2. Who might you talk with about this event (immediate family, neighbors, teachers, or others)?
3. When do you plan on talking with them? If you are using teachers as sources, think ahead. You will most likely need to set up an appointment with them soon.
4. What questions can you ask them to get the conversation going?

John's list of events (see Figure 3.3) starts off with a host of national conflicts: WWI, WWII, Korea, Vietnam, the Gulf War, the second Gulf War (Iraq), 9/11,

history project Rough Rough Draft
    The Day My Grandpa snuck
on a ~~B~~ B-24 liberator A few Days
After D-Day.
    20 historic events
1. WWI   19. MLK ussiniation
2. WWII   20. March on washington
3. Korea
4. Vietnam
5. Gulf war
6. 2nd Gulf war (present war)
7. 9/11
8. Civil Rights movement
9. Civil war
10. Great Depression
11. Sighing of the Declaration of independence
12. cold war
13. Assination of Lincoln
14. Assisation of JFK
15. Underground railroad
16. Berlin air lift
17. hiroshima
18. nagissaki

Figure 3.3. John's Historic Events

the Cold War. He also includes other events that captured the social movement of the late twentieth century. John's task will be to think about these events, to consider whose story he wants to explore, and to begin planning for his information gathering.

Plans for Day Two, Nonfiction Unit (day four of the semester)	
Time	**Tasks**
12:05–12:30	Hand out cards for heterogeneous grouping. Share newspaper articles and poems for fastwrite and discussion in new groups.
12:30–12:50	*Night* quiz. Sharing significant quotes.
12:50–1:05	Short lesson on power words and paragraphing.
1:05–1:25	Jump-in reading of *Night*.
1:25–1:35	Sharing of events since 1930.
1:35–1:40	Sharing of Nonfiction Writing Initial Information Sheet.

Day Three, Nonfiction Unit

As students take their cards, enter, and find their new groups, an overhead transparency is waiting with the first writing invitation of the day. This will be a short class, less than an hour in length, so work begins as the students walk in the door.

Writing Invitation 4

First, return to your page of power words. Look at the words you have included and look over your readings. Make observations about words and paragraphs you have noted.

Next, return to your reading and add words that you want to start integrating into your writing and speech on the power words sheet.

Reminder: clip your power words sheet into the front of your notebook.

Finally, describe what you noticed about Wiesel's paragraphs.

When the class convenes as a whole, they discuss paragraph observations, noting that interesting paragraphs vary in length—just like interesting sentences. Wiesel's varied length of paragraphs speeds the reader up or slows the reader down.

Christopher remarks that he has been told that a paragraph must have between four and six sentences and must always have a topic sentence, giving Tracy a teachable moment to draw attention to published authors who, like Wiesel, allow meaning—not arbitrary formulas about length—to dictate the length of a paragraph.

Stan notes how some of Wiesel's paragraphs offer sparse information and then quickly move on to new material. As an example, he notes the scene where the prisoners have petrol thrown over them before they enter the shower, and he reports that in some of these situations, he has difficulty picturing the events, leaving him wanting more. This allows Stan and others to think about how an author relies on the background knowledge of readers and how such reliance can be a problem if the reader is not as familiar with the time period.

Other passages are described: the killing of babies; the scene of the march when prisoners end up in a pile on top of one another clamoring at dead flesh to get out and escape suffocation; the scenes on the train where only a portion of the people could sit. Students recall their own explode-a-moment writings, and point to passages where Wiesel uses this technique; they observe how the story is carried along on carefully selected episodes that are "exploded" in this way. From every corner of the classroom, students examine the text and identify techniques the writer uses, and they discuss which of these techniques work best for them as readers and which they will want to consider modeling in their own writing.

"Why do you think some of us are drawn to one passage and others to different ones?" Tracy asks. Students consider this and talk about how their different backgrounds probably make them think about different things. Tracy nods and explains how "a book is just a collection of text—the meaning is waiting to be made by the reader." While she does not speak of transactional theory or literary theorist Louise Rosenblatt, Tracy does show the significance of transaction between a reader and a text, describing how it is not only *who* we are as readers that determines the interpretation we make of a piece of literature, but which critical lens we use to interpret texts. Tracy explains that the lenses we wear as we read actually reflect literary theories, and that most of us use more than one as we read any particular passage. Drawing on the work of Deborah Appleman (2000), Tracy shares definitions of three literary theories—Historical Criticism, Feminist Criticism, and Marxist Criticism.

> *Historical Criticism:* Using this theory requires that you apply to a text specific historical information about the time during which an author wrote. History, in this case, refers to the social, political, economic, cultural, and/or intellectual climate of the time.
> *Feminist Criticism:* A feminist critic sees cultural and economic disabilities in a patriarchal society that have hindered or prevented women from realizing

their creative possibilities and women's cultural identification as a merely negative object, or "Other," to man as the defining and dominating "Subject." *Marxist Criticism:* A Marxist critic grounds theory and practice on the economic and cultural theory of Karl Marx and Friedrich Engels. . . . [T]his school of critical theory focuses on power and money in works of literature. (155–56)

"Each of these lenses," Tracy explains, "helps us make sense of text, and applying a different lens will help us see new things or think about things we've seen in different ways." Her explanation further illuminates the class's earlier discussion about powerful words and paragraphs.

Attention turns to the small groups. Although together in class for five days, some still do not know each other's names. To better introduce themselves to others in their writing group, they are asked to discuss this question: "Do you think that the world will be a better or worse place in 100 years?" (Stock 1987, 16). While the students converse, Tracy looks over each student's Nonfiction Writing Initial Information Sheet assigned at the last class.

After much thought, John has decided to focus his writing on Vietnam, interview a family friend who had been there during the Vietnam conflict, and weave his biographical account around this individual's experiences. Lily has chosen to work with her grandmother, a victim of polio during a national epidemic, and reveal through her writing the human side of this terrifying disease. Barry has discovered a family story from the days of Prohibition while Celly has chosen to immerse herself in an insider's account of 9/11, recounting the event from the perspective of a firefighter who was involved firsthand in the events of the day. Because of his own family's background as immigrants from Turkey, Christopher is uniquely positioned to open up the story of political suppression while Zane has uncovered an amazing family story that emerged from a horrible accident in which his grandfather caused the death of the great-grandfather. Topics around the classroom reflect the varied stories that emerge from unique student interests.

As the class reconvenes, Tracy nudges the conversation back to *Night*, to what Elie Wiesel has left when all of his material things are gone: his father and his will to survive. She shares poignant personal stories about moments in her own life that are so integrally a part of her that she could never lose them, intense moments with her grandmother, now deceased, and her young daughter. She describes how writing about those moments makes them even more special, and explains how her connection with *Night* is about going back to the essentials, to what is most important in her own story. She encourages students to select a time or an event that is important to them for the focus of their own nonfiction piece, and then she shares the following assignment sheet.

Writing Assignment 4: Nonfiction Writing

Elie Wiesel's novel *Night* is a superb model for nonfiction writing. He captures the reader from the first page to the last. He puts individual faces on history. Through him, we finish the book with a deeper understanding of what it meant to live through the Holocaust. We will use Wiesel's writing as a model for our own. We will study his sentence structure, word choice, paragraphs, and story development.

My hope is that you can follow in Wiesel's footsteps; you will take a piece of history and put an individual face on it. This will take some time. You will need to select the historical event you want to focus on, and then you will have to talk to people to find "the story" that you want to tell.

The conversation phase of this will most likely take time. Don't procrastinate! Simply interviewing someone about history is not sufficient. You are looking for the stories behind the historical event. The individual stories are what put faces on history. If you wanted facts you could do a Google search or look in an encyclopedia. For this assignment, you need to sit down, listen, listen some more, and wait for the story. Be patient. You want the story.

When you are done with your piece of writing, you should be ready to share it with the person whose story you told.

Students are encouraged to begin work on their piece over the weekend and are reminded they will have writing workshop time the following week, too.

Today's class is shorter than the other two for the week, so students move quickly to the end-of-the-week Round Table for announcements, thanks, and apologies. They have done this only once so far this semester, but all seem to anticipate this end-of-the-week ritual. Tracy encourages students to begin their primary and secondary research immediately, reading about the time period and specific event that will be the context for their work, and by talking with the individual whose story will be shared. She answers questions about the nonfiction writing assignment and encourages students to come to their next class on Tuesday with notes as they will begin scheduling dedicated blocks of time for workshop next week. Further, she assures students that they will work together to generate the rubric for the nonfiction paper.

The sense of community in the class is evident today with thanks voiced for rides home, for help in class, for support on a project. Students share important news—a date to a Sadie Hawkins dance at one school; a homecoming date at another; a conference at a local university; an upcoming college tour. Quick, warm, supportive . . . and out the door for a weekend.

Taking a Step Back

The poetry Tracy chose to begin the thematic unit immediately took students to the horror of the events and places associated with the Holocaust as seen through

Plans for Day Three, Nonfiction Unit (day five of the semester)	
Time	**Tasks**
1:30–2:00	Hand out cards for heterogeneous grouping. Writing Invitation 4. Discussion of power words and paragraphs. Introduction of literary criticism to text.
2:00–2:15	Small group discussion of prompt.
2:15–2:30	Whole group Round Table.

the eyes of children. We are reminded of the often overlooked importance of re-reading literature (Blau 2003; Beers 2003). Hearing lines of a poem or story once offers an idea of what the work may be about. Hearing them a second or third time, and possibly from another reader, helps students to think about significant lines and images and to become more immersed in the message of the piece.

Reading is an active process of meaning making, and students should be given an opportunity to crystallize their own understanding of a work before engaging in more public discourse about it (Rosenblatt 1976). By encouraging students to think about the varied ways one might respond to a poem or story, Tracy helps situate meaning making as a personal choice a reader makes and validates the many ways students have for connecting to texts. Giving them that choice makes it possible for Barry to respond with words, Celly with a drawing, and John with lyrics to a song.

Tracy helps to establish a context for understanding the events associated with the Holocaust in a number of ways. One strategy, creating a KWL chart that draws out what students know (K), what questions they have (W), and what they have learned (L), allows them to share their knowledge about the Holocaust. Students who may have no knowledge are able to begin building a context for their reading and thinking, making it more likely that they will be drawn into the book that will initiate the unit's nonfiction study. If the KWL chart is posted in the classroom, it will be possible to add to the information that is known as students learn more. The KWL also allows for students to venture a query about the topic at hand—*I think this is a fact, but I'm not sure*. This, too, is valuable because it raises awareness of things to pay attention to as students read and discuss texts.

Reading aloud to students has been demonstrated repeatedly to be an important strategy for drawing them into texts, filling their ears and brains with well-articulated language, and introducing an author's style (Beers 2003; Allen 1995). When Tracy reads aloud, she occasionally stops, drawing attention to a word or a series of sentences and helping students softly develop their sense of good writing. Occasionally, she exclaims with pleasure when she encounters a phrase or image that is particularly rich. For some of the readers in her class, this is very important because they struggle with reading. It is helpful to be drawn into the story and to see its unique qualities and thought-provoking aspects through another's eyes.

Tracy uses quick timed reading to accomplish several things. It allows her to gauge the approximate reading speed of each student, making it possible for her to work with them to set realistic reading goals for each day so they will be able to get through the text in the required amount of time (Beers 2003). It permits Tracy to identify her struggling students quickly so that she can plan individual interventions and supports as they move into their first whole class reading experience. Moreover, this early check helps students to reflect on their own needs for pacing and support, raising their metacognitive awareness of their reading process.

As students leave class today, they are already thinking ahead to important contemporary historical events. Scaffolding the selection of a topic in this way helps to build interest and ownership as students move toward creating individual nonfiction pieces in the coming weeks.

The rich set of text materials—a book-length memoir, poetry, newspaper articles, and various human experiences associated with the Holocaust—supports connections between global circumstances and the deeply personal ones affecting Wiesel and the Jewish people caught up the horrors of WWII. In addition, by encouraging students to think about their own reactions if forced to flee their homes due to happenings beyond their control, Tracy helps them to personalize the events they are studying and to bring them on to the current global stage. Being a refugee, a victim of abuse on a large scale, is as much a contemporary reality as it was an historical one, a circumstance made ever more poignant in the aftermath of Hurricane Katrina. As these students "crystalize their own understanding" (Rosenblatt 1978), they do so with encouragement to think beyond their own needs and interpretations to those of others, both within their immediate social context and in contexts beyond their own.

As students move forward to creating their own nonfiction pieces, the multiple representations of nonfiction genres introduced in the Holocaust study will be enhanced with print and electronic secondary research materials, historical fiction, and more. These broad readings allow students to develop a multifaceted picture of the time, place, and circumstance associated with a particular event.

For many teens, the world can seem an overwhelming place. At many junctures these students are encouraged to think critically, making connections between texts, shared experiences, and the world. Critical literacy requires that the individual use her literacy to see the world differently, to act on her new understandings, to change the world. By thinking carefully and critically, young adults will be better prepared to carry their new understandings into their worlds, imagining new possibilities for a future they help to sculpt. Hopefully, they will develop a more defined awareness that their literacy matters because they—and their voice—matter (Yagelski 2000).

Ownership of learning is clearly a significant part of this classroom's curriculum. As demonstrated by the multiple invitations to draw on the information being shared in class, students are encouraged to take charge of the strategies and skills taught to improve their writing. The short focus on power words is one example. Instead of preteaching vocabulary or offering lists of words that the teacher selects and the students study for a test, a strategy shown time and again to be unsuccessful (Sipe 2003; Allen 1999), students gather words from their reading that they want to learn and to use in their own writing. Individual, small group, and, sometimes, whole group lessons share strategies for doing so, and students are expected to select a strategy that works for them to remember the words. This approach acknowledges that we learn differently from one another and that this variation is okay.

Engaging students in oral reading can be a powerful strategy in secondary classrooms. Not only does oral reading build interest in a text, it also supports students' ability to visualize the story and improves their sense of story and sentence structure (Anders and Levine 1990). Because the vocabulary found in *Night* includes many precise and uncommon words, it becomes even more helpful for challenged readers to hear those words in the context of the story, to build their understanding of the story as a support for their continued silent reading (Beers 2003). Jump-in reading allows challenged readers to hear and envision the story with the support of multiple voices. As structured, the jump-in strategy allows students to read aloud as much or as little as they wish. For some, their contribution may be several paragraphs; for others, it may be as little as a sentence. Because unrehearsed oral reading may be highly stressful for some, this strategy becomes particularly valuable in the high school setting. In all cases, voices are honored and ownership for the shared experience is encouraged.

Throughout their reading experiences, students' opportunities to connect, to make sense of, and to respond to texts from individual perspectives are scaffolded in many ways, including generating lists of possible ways to respond and engaging in multiple small and whole group response activities. In addition, Tracy introduces them to a variety of lenses to help them view the worlds they are exploring with new eyes. For many, this is new territory; they have not engaged in critical literacy in this way before, and the experience sensitizes them, helping them think about situations and circumstances in new ways and inviting further personal response as they strive and struggle to accommodate new perspectives with their own.

In these first days of the nonfiction study, opportunities for students to reflect are around every corner. What do you know? What information have you learned? What do you think? Wearing this lens, how does your thinking change? What are the characteristics of good nonfiction writing? Time after time, ownership for thinking is given to the students, and they rise to the occasion—contributing in groups, helping to build a base of whole class knowledge, shaping the criteria that will become a rubric for writing.

Further, the sense of community deepens. Extending the first two days of class when community building was paramount, the continuous sifting into new groups, the daily opportunities to know one another and share a variety of types of writing, and the end-of-the-week Round Table for thanks and apologies, all build ownership for the group, a willingness to support the individual, and a sense of pervasive camaraderie.

4

Shaping Original Works of Nonfiction

Day Four, Nonfiction Unit

A fast-paced class, Day Four of the unit starts with a very different look at non-fiction as Tracy asks students what they know about the famous speech "I Have a Dream" by Dr. Martin Luther King. With copies of the speech in every student's hands, they begin a jump-in reading, Tracy reading first. As with earlier jump-in readings, individuals read as far as they wish, pause, and then another voice takes over. Once through the speech, it is time to pause and reflect. Tracy asks the students to look in their notebooks at the list of ways to respond to literature that they generated the first day of their nonfiction study. Together, they now expand that list to include new ideas.

- Put ideas into a plan of action.
- Do a demonstration or protest.
- Write a short piece as if you are a member of Dr. King's audience.
- Do a dramatic reading of selected parts that you think are most important.
- Write a script.
- Rewrite for current society update.
- Attend or give a lecture on a similar issue.
- Pose questions: What if everyday all of us read this speech and attempted to live that day like the speech suggests?

Students select one of the ways to respond, flip to the front of their notebooks where daily writing invitations are collected, and spend five minutes responding to Martin Luther King's speech.

As soon as the responses are complete, students turn to the members of their new groups, introduce themselves in case there's anyone in the group who does not know them, and share their responses. When they reconvene as a whole class, several students share. For example, Christopher wrote

> I stood there, among others, all contained within a glacier of bodies. Except our glacier was not moving; we stood as one, mesmerized by Martin Luther King's words. "I have a dream," he said, and these words in particular reached out to me for so did I. Though I had always asked foolish questions about our freedom, it had never made sense to me, until now.
>
> "Let freedom ring," I wanted to get out there, today, with bells and whistles or just my voice, and let everyone know how I felt, or rather, how I, and everyone around me, should be. My mother was shouting out words that I could not hear, for I was blind, deaf, and dumb to all but my ears chose to receive.

Rebecca, drawn to the powerful language of the speech, selects significant words and phrases from the poem and arranges them to look and read like a poem.

> Free at last
> to pray together
> to struggle together
> to go to jail together
> I have a dream.
>
> Transformed!
> Join hands and
> walk together as
> sisters and brothers.
> Hew out a stone of hope.
> Transform the jangling discords!
> We will be free one day.
>
> My country 'tis of thee.
> Transformed into an oasis of
> freedom and justice,
> judged not by the color of their skins
> Let freedom ring!
> Thank God Almighty!
> Free at last!

One after the other, students share and then turn their attention to specific lines that resonate for them—lines that stand out from the rest.

> With this faith we will be able to work together, pray together, to struggle together, to go to jail together, to stand up for freedom together, knowing that we will be free one day.
> Free at last, free at last. Thank God Almighty, we are free at last!

I have a dream today.

We cannot walk alone.

We cannot be satisfied as long as the Negro's basic mobility is from a smaller ghetto to a larger one.

And finally, they move back to notebooks to capture their emerging thoughts on King's speech.

> To me, this speech is very powerful. It involves great words from a great man, urging others to dream as he had done. On a different note, when I read this, it shows me the many years in the fight for racial equality. MLK's metaphors are a bit extensive in use, but they help to convey the hardships felt by all present. (Christopher)

Tracy reminds them of the benefits of multiple readings, asks that they review the speech for their next class to see if there's a part or two they particularly like, and encourages them to practice it for the subsequent rereading at their next class on Thursday. They will focus this second reading on writing style to examine some of the ways that King makes the speech dramatic and compelling with an eye to modeling some of the techniques in their own writing.

The class talks about the growing number of writing invitations in the front of their notebooks. These, Tracy explains, are kernels that can be grown into full pieces if the author chooses. On the other hand, many fastwrites will remain unfinished, perhaps to be revisited in the future. She reminds students that it is okay to stop a piece that isn't working. Writers do this all the time.

Before shifting their attention back to the final pages of *Night*, the class looks once again at the growing list of things they know about the Holocaust. Though the reading of the novel has encouraged an aesthetic reading, one designed to support personal connection to the story and understanding of the plight of the people caught up in the horror of the time and events, nonetheless abundant information has been gathered through the reading. Without ever telling the students to read for particular facts, they have, in fact, discovered much significant information. Their collaborative list continues to grow as they add the following.

What We've Learned About the Holocaust
1. Most engaged in manual labor and were killed if they couldn't.
2. Prisoners had different levels of responsibility within the camps. Some were promoted to rule over the other prisoners. Not just Nazis supervised.
3. "Kaddished"—said to themselves.
4. The handicapped and mentally disabled were discriminated against.

5. They were put in ghettos before being shipped off to camps.
6. Germany started to teach about the Holocaust in schools about a year ago! (Personal knowledge brought to the class by a student whose family comes from Germany.)
7. People who were blind, deaf, or had genetic diseases were involuntarily sterilized.
8. The ideal of perfection was the Aryan race.
9. Gold teeth and all other possessions were taken.
10. Surprised at the availability of hospitals. Didn't realize that the prisoners had any medical care.
11. Officers were sometimes guilty of raping women and children.
12. The liberation of Buchenwald came with the arrival of the American tanks.
13. Surprised by brief moments of humanity demonstrated by individuals.
14. Astonished by the total number of people killed and that any actually survived.

Tracy begins the final read aloud, the words of the stark horror of the final days of the Holocaust suspending themselves in the room. Students are motionless. Exceptional readers and challenged readers alike listen intently as the story grips them. Her voice softens and slows as she reads the final scene.

> Three days after the liberation of Buchenwald I became very ill with food poisoning. I was transferred to the hospital and spent two weeks between life and death.
> One day I was able to get up, after gathering all my strength. I wanted to see myself in the mirror hanging on the opposite wall. I had not seen myself since the ghetto.
> From the depths of the mirror, a corpse gazed back at me.
> The look in his eyes, as they stared into mine, has never left me. (109)

With the final words of the novel, it is now time for students to react using the type of response or critical lens they choose. There are no questions before they begin writing. Hardly a sound is heard in the room save the scratch of pens on paper. Heads are bent toward their own emerging words as students crystallize their responses and reactions to the horror that was the Holocaust—now a very personal response.

> The first time I realized that the Holocaust happened to my people was when I was 10. I told my dad I wanted a tattoo of a butterfly on my back. I knew he would say no, but what he told me about why he never wanted me to get a tattoo was something that will remain in me forever. He said his mother had had

a tattoo. He said she had a number on her inner arm. He said she hadn't wanted the tattoo and she had been forced to be branded with the serial number the Nazis had tattooed on my grandmother. (Elizabeth)

The author of *Night*, Elie Wiesel, has put together a masterpiece of writing. It was so dramatic and to the point it made you feel like you were another prisoner writing down all of Wiesel's thoughts. I am a very visual person; I try to picture everything I read. This made for a very, very intense and moving book. The end was especially evocative, and I think I will carry those last two sentences with me for the rest of my life. (Zane)

I found it interesting that the ideas of what was or was not important changed throughout the period of time in the book. At the beginning what was important was staying together as a family. But as time progressed, other factors came into play and became more prevalent. For example, Eli's friend left his father because he was just something in the way. Food became more important, and right at the end people were willing to push possible friends, who might or might not be dead, over the side of the train for more food. (Stan)

From responding and sharing, the students are nudged to look again at the writing itself, to think of the ways both Wiesel and King have elicited responses through particular skills in manipulating language. Students volunteer a number of qualities the two very different pieces of writing share: varied sentence structure; selected examples of repetition; the powerful emotions evoked by the use of detail; the personal connection that develops with the use of the first person "I." Such discussions always include encouragement to experiment with similar techniques in their own writing. An update on their nonfiction piece is due at the next class—a very rough draft to help Tracy see where they are in the process and what types of problems they may be encountering with the writing. She reminds them that they will be telling a story that will share a moment in history.

Just before leaving for the day, they quickly brainstorm a list of observations about nonfiction writing and which techniques are important to this type of writing. Students contribute the following.

Observed Characteristics of Strong Nonfiction Writing
- includes the use of metaphors
- observes injustices and writes about them
- includes a purpose that is clear
- both expresses individual perspectives and a feeling of a larger societal concern
- uses powerful imagery
- uses carefully selected descriptive words and phrases

- descriptive paragraphs often end with flat declarative statements
- demonstrates dramatic flow of sentences: scattering of long/short sentences and paragraphs
- uses repetition of selected words, parallel sentences
- relates facts through personal accounts using first-person or third-person omniscient narration

This list will provide the foundation for fashioning the rubric to be used for discussing rough drafts of the student nonfiction pieces and, ultimately, for both self-assessment and teacher assessment of the assignment. Tracy reminds students to bring along their work-in-progress tomorrow so that she can see how their nonfiction pieces are progressing and so they can make good use of the workshop time that is planned.

Plans for Day Four, Nonfiction Unit (day six of the semester)	
Time	**Tasks**
12:05–12:30	Hand out cards for heterogeneous grouping. Add to list of ways to respond to a text. First reading of "I Have a Dream" by Martin Luther King.
12:30–12:50	Individual written responses. Small group sharing.
12:50–1:25	Return to KWL for Holocaust facts. Complete oral reading of *Night*.
1:25–1:40	Response to *Night*. Begin developing rubric for nonfiction papers.

Day Five, Nonfiction Unit

Much of today's class (day five of the unit) is devoted to workshop time, as students continue the process of developing and shaping their nonfiction pieces. As the class comes together, they revisit "I Have a Dream" with another jump-in reading. Tracy starts and seven students, in turn, assume voices in the delivery of the speech. "Pick out one line that you feel to be particularly powerful," she instructs the students. Lines are cited verbatim in the front section of the writer's notebooks before students share their choices and think together about why certain types of language stand out as being more moving and more interesting than others.

Moving quickly to a fastwrite, students spend five minutes responding to the following writing invitation.

Writing Invitation 5

What does this speech mean? How could this be a guide for living now? What do you take away from it? What can you learn from it?

Students are accustomed to these moments set aside to capture quick thoughts on paper. Soon, they turn to their new group, introduce themselves, and share responses. This predictable procedure is now a trusted method for breaking the ice, building fluency, and engaging ideas.

Moving from small group to whole group, once again they share their lines, this time moving from student to student around the classroom, an exercise reminiscent of the first day when they sat together, hands on the web, feeling the quick pulse in the line as it moved around the group. This quick sharing provides a frame for observations about rich language. Students look back at the list of ten features they generated yesterday, and collaboratively they added new observations about quality writing.

Characteristics of Strong Writing

- some lines have deeper meaning that inspires reflection about humanity and introspection about personal issues
- the writing sometimes goes beyond the text itself, suggesting connections to other things or books or events
- lots of variation in punctuation including use of commas, periods, quotes, colons, semicolons, hyphens, dashes, question marks, exclamation points
- lots of attention to detail. When a writer uses a fragment or incorrect subject-verb agreement, it's usually clear that they did it for a reason.
- spelling is cleaned up

They add additional information to the list by looking back at the beginning section of *Night* to revisit some of the stylistic decisions made by Wiesel.

- use of snapshots and thoughtshots (Lane 1993)
- sometimes reduces large amounts of time to very few words: shrink a century (Lane 1993)
- sometimes slows down the action to give lots of details about a small amount of time: explode a moment (Lane 1993)
- sometimes uses specific techniques for handling time, details, sentence and paragraph structure (e.g., repeat use of fragments)

Tracy hands back their original explode-a-moment papers and asks students to reread their earlier work with their list of qualities of good writing in mind. She explains that we often make the same types of errors over and over until we are able to see them for ourselves and take ownership for our own writing. In short, she encourages them to become their own editors. To start, they are asked to take these early pieces of writing and read them as editors: revising a sentence or paragraph as needed; importing a particular writing device; varying sentence or paragraph structure. They are encouraged to mark up their papers: crossing out words, restructuring paragraphs, drawing arrows to show where new language will be inserted. To support this work, they review a list of editing notations that will provide a code to direct later revision. In addition to the list of writing features they have just developed, they have the skills and craft lessons in their notebooks for reference.

With these tools, they attempt to "mark up" their papers for appropriate revision and editing. The goal is to train the eye to notice and appreciate excellent writing and apply this new appreciation to one's own work.

Zane's original piece places the reader directly into the drama of a first race.

Zane's First Draft

HOOOOOOOONK. Just as soon as it had started, the race was over, heralded with a sound every bit as loud as it was started with. My senses were flooded with information as the adrenaline wore off. The stands were screaming and cheering, the iron tang still in my mouth, I refocused on the back in front of me, and I could smell the river I was floating on. And the pain. Always the pain; in my arms, hands, legs, back, feet. But it would soon be gone, replaced with the weight from the medal around my neck.

His rewrite demonstrates refinement of his original skills and his growing awareness of technique encouraged by feedback from his writing partners and Tracy.

Zane's Second Draft

The gun blast cut the air like a knife. With the sound, 45 guys burst into action. Every thought flew out of my head except for take a stroke, take a stroke, take a stroke. All senses went on auto-pilot. Everything came down to muscle memory. Eyes rolling around, muscles already screaming, I knew I wouldn't make it to the end of the race. I could only hear the roaring of my blood and breath in my ears. I had to push, push until I didn't have anything left. A taste hit my mouth, the iron tang of lactic acid overflowing out of my protesting muscles. Just take a stroke, take a stroke, take a stroke . . .

It's important to note that this remarkable revision did not happen seamlessly. When Tracy first returned the papers with encouragement to "mark them up," she was disappointed to see how little students could own the process. With individuals and small groups, she revisited earlier minilessons on sentence structure, word choice, and more. The results of this deeper instruction paid off with more highly refined drafts.

As promised, this class period will provide a substantial block of time for writing. As students move into the workshop, some also move around the room—to more isolated corners for drafting; to the computers at the perimeter of the room for research, writing, and revising; to a quiet space by the bookcases in the back corner of the room for reading and conferencing. During this time, Tracy visits with individuals and conferences on emerging drafts; students also have the opportunity to seek an audience with a peer, checking whether a particular sentence or paragraph clearly expresses their intent. Students who have an urgent need to speak with Tracy request a time before she begins more routine visits with others.

Zane's nonfiction piece is producing elements of family history that prove to be both spellbinding and shocking. His early work has been largely focused on collecting biographical information. Zane's gathering of information uncovers a fascinating story that is likely to produce a strong impact on his readers.

Zane's Nonfiction Early Fact Search

[Great-grandpa was] born in Texas on a farm.
His grandfather was killed by his father in a hunting accident.
One day his uncle showed up on his door step, asking my great-grandma to marry him so he could take the family. Great-grandpa threatened to shoot him. Entire family moved to Washington and changed their names to Rose to escape his uncle and the Great Depression.

It also generates a host of questions.

- How did this situation happen?
- What were the details?
- Why did his grandfather choose to tell this story when he did?
- Why did he come to the United States?

The workshop provides the time, space, and support Zane needs to share his emerging work, receive feedback from several peers, and check in with Tracy for strategic advice.

As the class draws to a close, Tracy reminds students that workshop time will be an integral part of most of their classes now. It is their responsibility to bring their in-progress writing and research each day and to take ownership for the best use of the time.

Plans for Day Five, Nonfiction Unit (day seven of the semester)	
Time	**Tasks**
12:05–12:30	Hand out cards for heterogeneous grouping. Second reading of "I Have a Dream" by Martin Luther King. Writing Invitation 5 Selecting and sharing a special line from the speech. Response to writing invitation and sharing responses.
12:30–12:50	Further develop list of qualities of excellent writing. Mark up their own explode-a-moment pieces.
12:50–1:35	Writing workshop time.
1:35–1:40	Closing reminders.

Day Six, Nonfiction Unit

From the beginning of the semester, students have focused attention on effective words and sentence constructions. Today, as soon as they find their seats, Tracy asks them to open their notebooks to the power words section, to revisit Dr. King's speech a final time, and to look for words and sentences that particularly appeal to them. Soon, they are redirected to the writing invitation.

Writing Invitation 6
Write from the line: "I Have a Dream . . ." but in your piece write your own dream using at least two of the power words from your list and trying to imitate King's writing style.

Students share these fastwrites with their groups along with group introductions as needed. Once again, they are asked to read their writing exactly as written instead of just describing it (see Figure 4.1). Each group encourages one or more of its members to share their piece with the class as a whole; Tracy keeps a watchful eye to be sure all the students are having opportunities to have their voices heard.

Students will have an entire week between this class and the due date for their nonfiction papers because of the interruption of winter break. Tracy provides a rubric that has grown from their shared observations; this will serve as their guide for the development and assessment of the papers. As they look over the rubric, she

Death is indeed a slave's
freedom,
but it's also a curse,
a curse that you will never
be able to see your brothers
and your sisters walk out of
a door that was their own and
not have to worry about a damn
thing except wilin' away the
hours of a lazy Sunday.

—Zack, poem

Dr. King had a dream
that he'd like to have seen.
He said to his people
we better do our thing
to make our world a better place
for our kids to live.
He wanted his speech to have an impact,
and it did.

He was talking about
race, religion, and the
quality of life.
Discrimination
segregation
just ain't right.
His people were oppressed
and that's not cool.
They made a shit load of ruckus
because they thought they were tools.

You moved the masses
with hope and fears
but who has answered
your people's tears?
You gave your people hope.
They thought it was dope.
But still nothing has been done . . .

42 years later
everything is the same.
Nobody is willing to
play the equal rights game.
White men still suck,
it gets worse by the hour.

Figure 4.1. Responses to Writing Invitation 6

Where are your people now
Screaming black power! black power!
Your message was lost
somewhere along the way.
Who's left on the list
to point your finger and blame.
Your intentions were good
but no one really thought you would
have your morals and
values forgotten in the
ripples of time.
You moved the masses
with hope and fears
but who has answered
your people's tears?
You gave your people hope.
They thought it was dope.
But still nothing has been done . . .

      —Zack, original rap

It is obvious today that America has defaulted on this promissory note inso-
far as her citizens of color are concerned. Instead of honoring this sacred ob-
ligation, America has given the Negro people a bad check which has come
back marked "insufficient funds." This speech describes to me the injustices
that people face because of the cruelty of discrimination. Dr. King envisioned
a place free from brutality and racial inequality; he saw that today's world was
overcome by hate based upon trivial issues (the color of a person's skin). It
makes me think of how we as a nation can be so cruel to one another, and
even though people made efforts to change their ways, there will always be
hate, discrimination, and inequality to some degree. Dr. King's words are descriptive and powerful and they paint images in my mind of Dr. King's stand
at a podium, raising his voice to give people, suffering from discrimination,
some hope to "march ahead."

      —Lauren

Figure 4.1. *Continued*

reminds them that these criteria are the ones that emerged from their discussions
and observations about good writing based on the samples they have read together.

  Using these criteria, Tracy will develop a rubric for the final papers (see Figure 4.2). Students are comfortable with the rubric, perhaps because they have had

This rubric emerged from the lists of criteria of good nonfiction writing that we generated together. Keep these criteria in mind as you complete your nonfiction drafts. When you turn in your rough and final drafts, I'll ask you to initial the appropriate boxes. In addition to marking the boxes, you will write a self-evaluation letter about your writing.

Criteria	4 Terrific!	3. Getting there!	2 Some evidence of criteria. Revision suggested.	1 Little evidence of criteria. Revision required.
Powerful language Use of language includes metaphors, powerful images, carefully selected words and phrases.				
Writers' craft Demonstrates skill in using craft techniques such as scattering of long and short sentence and paragraphs; repetition of selected words, phrases, and fragments; use of parallel structures; snapshots, thoughtshots, shrinking a century, exploding a moment.				
Setting a context Inspires reflection about issues; has a purpose that is clear; offers personal and societal (larger) concern; goes beyond the text itself, suggesting connections to other things, books, or events.				
Appropriate conventions Pays attention to details. When fragments or other nontraditional structures are used, it's clear they are used for a reason; lots of variation in punctuation including commas, periods, semicolons, hyphens, dashes, and end punctuation; correct use of quotations; cleans up spelling.				

Figure 4.2. Student Initiated Rubric

such an integral role in formulating it. In addition to the rubric in Figure 4.2, Tracy shares a rubric that she uses with many pieces of writing, regardless of the genre (see Figure 4.3). She points out how this general guide parallels many of the features the students themselves noted in their criteria. Taken together, these rubrics are intended to support students as they think about their emerging drafts with a view toward sharing with an audience.

Because this is the last class of the week, they will end their work with a class Round Table. As students meet in a circle, sitting on the floor, they share snippets about their plans for the winter break along with thanks for individual help provided by a peer, an apology to a group member for not paying enough attention to his paper, and another about coming to class late. The community continues to gel for this group as they move from not knowing names to developing a sense of deep support for one another as writers. With Tracy's trilling, "Do NOT forget your papers!" students head off for a week's break.

Plans for Day Six, Nonfiction Unit (day eight of the semester)	
Time	**Tasks**
1:30–1:45	Hand out cards for heterogeneous grouping. Exercise with power words and sentences.
1:45–2:10	Writing Invitation 6: "I Have a Dream." Sharing of writing with writing groups and samples with the class as a whole.
2:10–2:15	Review of the writing rubric for nonfiction
2:15–2:30	Round Table for thanks and apologies.

Taking a Step Back

With the unexpected move to the contemporary speech of Dr. Martin Luther King, students are given an opportunity to step outside of the events of the Holocaust to examine a response to oppression from another vantage point. They are also able to see how a writer could engage nonfiction from another genre. Clearly, telling a story that is true can draw on far more complex definitions of nonfiction than they had originally believed.

The use of Dr. King's famous speech also provides students the opportunity to draw on many of the skills and craft discussions they have experienced. Looking at the text of the speech for the use of effective words and images, considering the

This rubric applies to almost all genres of writing. Keep it in mind as you write. When you turn in your rough and final drafts, I'll ask you to initial the appropriate boxes. In addition to marking the boxes, you will write a self-evaluation letter about your writing.

	A Bravo	B Good	C Average	D Lacks evidence/missing
Ideas and content	Ideas are richly developed with details and examples.	Ideas and content are adequately developed through details and examples.	Ideas and content may be developed with limited details and examples.	Ideas and content are supported by few, if any, details and examples.
Mechanics	The writer uses effective sentence structure and precise word choices (power words, vivid verbs, colons, semicolons, etc.).	The writer uses appropriate and varied sentence structure and word choices.	The writer uses basic sentence structure and limited vocabulary to convey a simple message.	The writer uses awkward sentence structure and inadequate vocabulary, which interfere with understanding.
Development	The writing is engaging, original, clear, and focused.	The writing is reasonably clear, focused and well-supported.	The writing has some focus and support.	The writing has little focus and development.
Organization	Organization and form enhance the central idea or theme; ideas are presented coherently to move the reader through the text.	Organization and form are appropriate, and ideas are generally presented coherently	The writing may be somewhat disorganized or too obviously structured.	There is little discernible shape or direction.

Figure 4.3. Tracy's Writing Rubric

© 2006 by Rebecca Bowers Sipe and Tracy Rosewarne from *Purposeful Writing: Genre Study in the Secondary Writing Workshop*. Portsmouth, NH: Heinemann.

use of repetition as a rhetorical device, and thinking about the various connections in the speech to events of the time and those that precede and follow it, students are able to identify myriad techniques that make writing effective and memorable.

It is easy to assume that knowledge of one genre is sufficient for success in other genres. While some knowledge is certainly transferable, each genre has distinctive characteristics that suggest both possibilities and constraints for the reader and writer. As Tracy's students move into the broad category of nonfiction, she understands the importance of immersing them in various types of nonfiction writing. Through reading and discussion experiences, students are then able to construct mental models that help them visualize the ways in which specific nonfiction genres work.

- What patterns of organization are possibilities?
- How does the author address the reader?
- How do elements like precise vocabulary, use of particular rhetorical devices, and choices about style come into play with a particular genre?
- What about conventions? When is it okay not to follow standard usage?

Reading and discussion provide rich opportunities for students to focus on how an author uses language for effect and provides the platform for thinking about genre as a choice that an author makes. Would Wiesel's account have been as powerful if written as a news story? A report? A traditional autobiography? Why was a memoir the perfect choice for this story? This type of thinking is important for Tracy's students, particularly as they move toward identifying a story they themselves will investigate and tell. With an array of nonfiction genre possibilities, they will need to be able to make conscious choices about the genre(s) they will employ to communicate their selection.

Earlier we visited two differing views: one, that certain writing considerations be first taught to give young writers clear direction about organizing their writing in unfamiliar genres, and the other that resists privileging certain writing considerations over others. Here, instead of prescriptive approaches, students are given opportunities to read, examine, and investigate exceptional pieces of writing and, as a result, to generate their own lists of qualities of good writing. Building from student observations, such lists provide a pathway to internalizing these qualities in ways that go far beyond imposing formulaic organizational patterns. Further, by immediately practicing the use of these qualities in their own frequent daily writing and in their more carefully developed bigger pieces, these students have multiple and ample opportunities to experiment with and internalize these qualities as they train both their eyes and ears to good writing.

Investigation into the conventions of a genre also provides the opportunity for students to contextualize their understanding of the various skills and craft lessons that Tracy provides. Each of these lessons has been crafted in response to needs identified in her students' early and ongoing fastwrites. Because each represents an area of identified need and each will be immediately reinforced in their writing, there is no sense of learning unimportant minutia divorced from meaningful tasks.

Moreover, it is clear that Tracy understands that there is a vast difference between reading in a new or unfamiliar genre and writing in it. Anyone who has tried to launch into writing for a new audience and purpose and in a new genre might attest to the initial struggle. So, in addition to immersing students in a variety of nonfiction genres, Tracy tries to help them pay attention to the various qualities of the pieces. They experiment with ways authors speed up and slow down texts, but also the ways in which particular sentence constructions and particular rhetorical constructions such as repetition help the reader see and experience the message in specific ways. These are techniques that students can import into their own work.

Teaching like this takes time. The learning that takes place in the workshop environment is thoughtful, strategic, and deeply applied. Thoughtful? Think of the many times that students have been asked to step back and think, to make decisions, to develop judgments, to share observations. Strategic? Every lesson, whether a short micro- or minilesson or a quick revisit of a craft or skills lesson with an individual student, has grown from Tracy's analysis of her students' work.

By examining the writing that is completed throughout the semester, much of which is stored in the writer's notebook and other pieces in their writing folders, she has been able to isolate skills that students either need help with or need to push to the next level. This approach saves an enormous amount of time that might otherwise be devoted to revisiting concepts that students already know were she restricted to a prescribed sequence of study. The key is that Tracy, as the teacher, is aware of what her students need and, as a result, can consciously take ownership for fashioning lessons to address those needs.

Just as Tracy takes ownership for instruction, students take ownership for their writing because they have choice on many levels. The curriculum set the nonfiction focus for the semester. Beyond that, students experience a tremendous degree of choice for the genre they choose and the topic they will pursue. Each topic or area of interest will lead students to different types of primary and secondary research. As we saw with Zane's early work, the family investigation he pursues takes him into some unanticipated territory as he learns fascinating and unanticipated family history.

This degree of choice is not without problems, of course. Some students, like Lily, find their research interests do not lead to satisfying results, requiring them to rethink—and in her case—begin again on a topic that is more rewarding. Even at this stage it is clear that the nature of this work is leading to a high level of ownership and pride. With criteria and a rubric that grew from it alongside one that is provided by Tracy, students move into their winter break with tools to help them complete the near final drafts that are due upon return.

5

Emerging Drafts

Day Seven, Nonfiction Unit

Ann Arbor weather can affect lesson plans on a whim, and as break comes to an end snowy conditions provide an additional few days for students to develop their papers at home. On the Thursday when they finally come back together with solid first drafts (day seven of the unit) Tracy reviews their work, identifies numerous areas for instructional focus, and anticipates the need for a substantial block of workshop time to support revision and editing. In addition, she begins to lay the groundwork for the next few weeks when the workshop design will take on a more student-directed focus with choice reading and writing occupying most of the instructional time. This week's three class periods have been set aside for workshop to complete the final revision and editing process for the nonfiction papers.

Today, Tracy begins class with a skills review from the writer's notebooks. In two very succinct microlessons—short instructional interventions that are even more abbreviated than traditional minilessons—she introduces strategies to help students remember how to distinguish and spell troublesome homophones; reviews how to use dialogue, applying correct use of quotation marks; and demonstrates how to use punctuation such as colons and semicolons effectively to support sentence variation and effect. She encourages students to use these skills immediately as they continue writing and refining their nonfiction pieces.

Their task today is to hold a conference with themselves, to read their own papers with an editor's eye. To help with this, they review once again some basic editing notations, making sure these are readily available in the skills section of their notebooks. These tools will be used to capture their various editing conversations so they can revisit the thinking later.

How does one hold a conference with oneself? Tracy explains how the brain fills in and creates meaning, regardless of what is on the paper. This allows us to "see" things that aren't there when we read silently. For today's work, she encourages students to use a strategy of reading their papers aloud to themselves—softly, but saying every word on the page and listening to the words carefully. The task is to "mark up" their paper—a skill they have practiced with the earlier paragraphs—adding words, moving around ideas, marking places where a passage could be helped with the introduction of dialogue, a snapshot, a thoughtshot, or another device they've practiced.

When they have completed this process they will have nearly an hour to continue writing and revising drafts. This process of "marking up" drafts will be repeated in stages, depending on the needs of the writer, as the papers move through multiple revisions and toward final publication and sharing.

It is important to note that students struggle initially with this new responsibility. Many are accustomed to a teacher marking up and commenting on drafts; often, these comments are for evaluation rather than revision. By this point, all have become accustomed to receiving feedback and suggestions from others to support their revision and editing. The skills involved in honing one's ability to provide feedback to oneself are different, and responsibility shifts, placing ownership of these skills with the writer first.

Even with this shift to assume more responsibility for their own revision, writers do not work in a vacuum. Today, they have two opportunities to collaborate. In their small groups they share a sentence from their own papers that they like a great deal, discussing the features that they think make the sentence work particularly well. They also have a few minutes to seek assistance for one area that is troublesome or just not coming together as it should. Then, as a whole group the class listens as each member contributes a successful sentence; one by one students offer crisp descriptions, vivid actions, engaging sentence structures.

Short sharing sessions such as these sharpen the ear and the eye to potential. When reading one's own work during conferences with oneself, students then look and listen for instances in which a sentence could be tightened, tweaked a bit to add punch to the writing; where information may be needed to enhance the message; where the introduction of a learned technique could be imported to make a passage flow more professionally.

As they begin this final week's work on the first nonfiction papers for the semester, the students are at various stages of completion. Just as the nonfiction genres vary, so too do the length of the pieces, the number of drafts, and the need for support. Though there is no magic number given for either length or revisions, students internalize the message that the writing is important, that they are expected to use the time and support available to hone and rehone as needed, and that they have a fair amount of latitude in the ways they accomplish this.

Students move freely between writing and reading this week, as they will for much of the rest of the semester's workshop time. While this degree of individualization could be distracting and difficult to track, Tracy navigates the diverse activities and needs by drawing on a variety of management tools such as a record-keeping grid (see Appendix B) modified from Nancie Atwell's State of the Class (1998). Tracy's adaptation provides a page for each student that is used to chart needs and progress. These individual sheets are eventually used for feedback to students and parents. As students commence their work, she moves quickly from cluster to cluster, from individual to individual, holding conferences about a paper, gathering data about progress—a process she has used throughout the semester, hence a comfortable and familiar one to students.

In addition to the rubric provided before break, Tracy provides students with additional guidelines to help them as they put together their last draft.

1. Be sure to include a cover page with your name, the date, and the title.
2. Remember to use 12-point type and Times or a similar font.
3. Remember to double-space all pages.
4. Include all drafts, each dated and arranged in chronological order—newest to oldest.
5. Finally, remember that last drafts should be between 4–10 pages.

Students know to keep all drafts of their work. In addition, they keep track of the skills they have chosen to work on during the course of a particular piece of writing. As we look at the progression of two pieces, we'll be able to watch the evolution from idea to draft, and from refinement to refinement as students look at their own work with the eyes of a reader and as they make adjustments in response to feedback from others—peers, parents, subjects of the papers, as well as their teacher.

As I move around the class on this day, noting the various topics of papers, I'm astonished at the array. The research is vibrant and compelling as a result of the interest students have discovered in real events and people. In many cases, the subjects of the interviews continue to inform the research even as the papers develop, adding depth and interest. For example,

- Allison writes of the fight for independence in Algeria, the home for her father and grandfather before they immigrated to America. Her interviews with her father offer shafts of light into the history of her family.
- John chooses to write about D-Day, June 6, 1944. He develops his piece initially as a first-person account as he relates the story of Fred Kagan from

the "inside." Later, the story shifts its point of view as he needs to include more of the thoughts and feelings of other individuals who emerge.

- Barry dips into a piece of family history that surprises him, discovering a relative who made and ran illegal alcohol during the time of Prohibition. Told from the voice of a child who watched the parent's activity, the piece explores emotion and frustration emerging from a complex period of American history while giving the reader information about this time and family.

- In "Wide Awake and Dreaming," Christopher investigates and describes the misery and violence experienced by family and friends in 1960 when the Justice Party moved to squelch the rising of the People's Republican Party in Turkey, a more libratory power. Because of his family's separation from relatives who still live in Turkey, he is particularly interested in investigating this part of his family's history.

- Zane chooses to explore the history of his own family and discovers in the process a terrible secret that shaped the family's history and even the family's name.

- Lily discovers a rich cache of letters that leads her to interviews with her grandmother, a child victim of polio during the time of WWII.

- Linda recaptures her father's history emerging from a childhood in "The Projects" in New Hampshire. The biography provides the platform for the daughter to collect, examine, capture, and honor the story of a parent in a way that holds deep meaning for both.

Across the room, twenty-eight different historical, nonfiction pieces are emerging, varying by length and genre but sharing in the same high level of investment and pride. As papers are shaped toward a final draft, young writers illustrate a growing ability to take control of their writing and produce documents that are meaningful to themselves and others.

From the time she was quite young, Linda had heard her father talk about his childhood in "The Projects." When given the opportunity to research a recent historical event through primary and secondary research, she immediately thought about the time and place that was so instrumental to her father's development. Her first draft was a predictably messy affair, capturing what she knew already as supported by brief conversations with her dad, and mapping out topics and questions for which she would need further investigation to get to the heart of her account (see Figure 5.1).

As is clear from her early draft, Linda has interest in her topic and helps the reader to have interest, too. She begins the story with her dad's voice strongly present in a first-person account. Abruptly, on page two we find the story closing—but not really closing. An array of questions, snippets of information, and isolated single-word references illustrate her thinking about what more she needs to know.

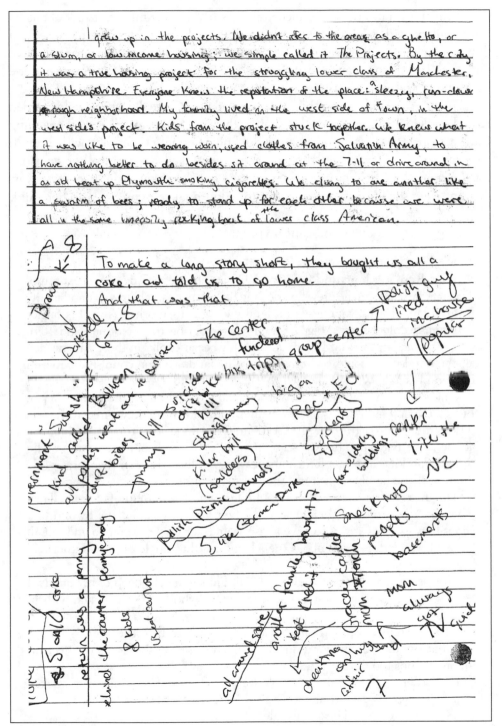

I grew up in the projects. We didn't refer to the areas as a ghetto, or a slum, or low income housing; we simple called it The Projects. By the city it was a true housing project for the struggling lower class of Manchester, New Hampshire. Everyone knew the reputation of the place: sleezy, run-down enough neighborhood. My family lived in the west side of town, in the west side's project. Kids from the project stuck together. We knew what it was like to be wearing worn, used clothes from Salvation Army, to have nothing better to do besides sit around at the 7-11 or drive around in an old beat up Plymouth smoking cigarettes. We cling to one another like a swarm of bees; ready to stand up for each other because we were all in the same uneasy feeling boat of the lower class American.

To make a long story short, they bought us all a coke, and told us to go home.
And that was that.

Figure 5.1. Linda's First Draft, Page 2

From the beginning of her piece, she has had opportunity to think about its development with peers and with Tracy. This week she brings in a more refined draft (see Figure 5.2). Though still handwritten, her account has grown to five pages, and from the many editing notes she has given herself, we see that she continues to rethink and revise it.

Though Linda identifies this as her second draft, it really isn't; she has added to and marked up at least one other draft as the story has grown, based on emerging information. Today, she works alone, holding a formal conference with herself. The suggestions for changes that she identifies today will go into her revisions for the draft that she'll bring with her to the next class meeting, two days away. At that time she'll select a peer editor for additional response to help her think about her final draft.

Zane has also done significant revision:

Zane's First Complete Draft

William Rose was born on May 23rd, 1929 in a house outside of San Antonio, Texas. A farmer's son, he grew up knowing little other than hard work and family loyalty. He was the youngest in a family of six: his mother Ann, his father William, his older sister Abigail, and his two older brothers Norman and Tom. A family that large was fairly common, mainly because folks in those days needed all the hands they could get to help with the land. To stop confusion between him and his dad, Will was known to everyone as Bill.

One night, once all the work was done and they had finished with supper, Bill's father brought all the kids together and told them he wanted to have a serious discussion with them. He sat them all down around the fire and looked at each one hard, like he was sizing them up. "Your all old enough now," he started, "and its time ya'll lerned about why we's livin' here in the states while the rest of the family is back in Denmark."

This has been a question all the children had been asking for years. They never got to see any of their relatives. Their friends would come by and talk about how exciting it was to have a visit from their uncle or granpa and tell all kinds of wonderful stories about the adventures that uncle or grandfather had been through.

"You see, this is hard for me to tell you. I'm the black sheep of my family. I have seven brothers and sisters and one mother who I haven't spoken with in almost twenty years, and it's cuttin' up my insides real bad. Your ma has known about this, and we reckon that your all old enough to hear the story."

What Bill did not know was just how much this story was going to affect his life in the not too distant future.

His father settled down, digging in for a long story. The children mimicked him, putting on a face that they hoped looked as serious as his. Bill's father cleared his throat and began this tale.

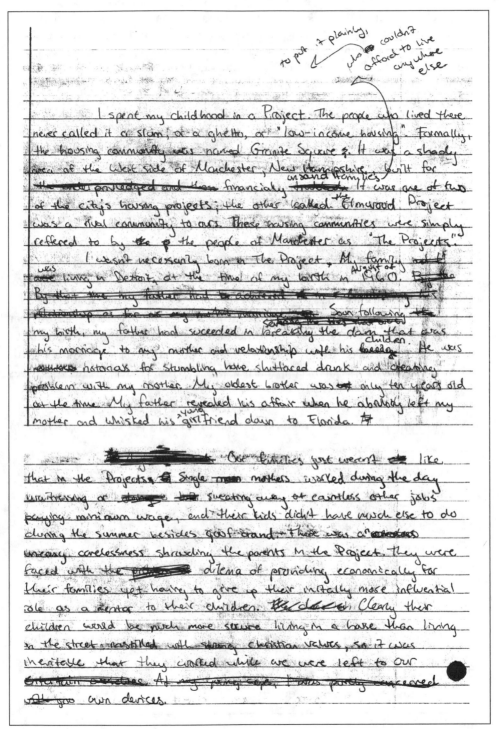

Figure 5.2. Linda's Second Draft

"Back when I was just a kid, about the age that Tom is, I was invited on a hunting trip with my father, grandfather, older brothers, and two of my uncles. This was back in Denmark, mind you, and it was easier to find larger game. We went up to forest about three days walk from our house and set up camp. I was having a grand time because I had finally been accepted into the group of men. This would be my first steps on the path of manhood."

"We went through two days without any trouble, my father and uncle both having killed a deer apiece. However, my father said that we couldn't go home without me first killing something, be it a rabbit, squirrel, or an elephant. So the next day I went out with a vengeance. I put everything I had learned from the men to use, all the techniques that had been passed down through the generations. I tried to hard. It made me tense. I got jumpy. My desire to kill something, anything, so that the men would take me seriously, made me slightly wild. Because I was so blind with desire, I shot my own father."

Despite rough edges and the unfinished nature of his draft, he manages to pull his reader into this unexpected family drama. Today he is ready for peer response. (see Figure 5.3). He'll ask his responders to read the story two ways: first as a reader with an eye toward what they want to hear more of, what parts they are unclear about, and where the story lacks coherence and clarity; then he'll want them to look at the piece through the lens of a writer. In both cases, either he or they will make notations directly on the paper so he'll have them handy as he continues his own revision.

As students culminate their work on this initial nonfiction study, Tracy is already looking ahead to the next week when they will transition into several

---

1. Select a peer revision partner whom you trust.
2. Schedule a mutually workable time to sit with that individual and review your piece.
3. While sitting with your partner, read your piece aloud for your revision partner.
4. Allow your revision partner to read through your piece silently and to make written suggestions directly on the paper.
5. Consider the possibility of working with an additional peer reviewer. Follow the same instructions as above.
6. When your peer review is complete, review all the comments and decide which, if any, you as the writer will act on.
7. Revise your piece once again based on the comments that you consider important for the overall quality.

Figure 5.3. Peer Review Process

weeks of open-ended reading and writing workshop. To prime the pump for this new study, she decides to talk about book recommendations today as she ends class. She shares a passage from *The Kite Runner* by Khaled Hosseini and encourages students to make recommendations of their own. In the past she has asked students initially to collect recommendations from individuals outside the class. By encouraging this personal, whole group sharing, though, she instantly creates a culture of readers.

Barry and Stan contribute new age titles as their current favorites: *Ishmael: An Adventure of the Mind and Spirit* by Daniel Quinn and *The Celestine Prophesy: An Adventure* by James Redfield. Abby jumps in with several sci-fi favorites. As categories of books begin to emerge, Tracy sets up five different discussion groups and students move quickly to the one representing their favorite genre or author, notebooks in hand. For fifteen minutes, the room hums with book talk, and no doubt the conversations could have extended for another half hour or more if time allowed. Only once did Tracy feel a need to jump in, joining the fiction group to help encourage more sharing and to round out the list by adding that, "If you like Jay Bennett's *I Never Said I Loved You*, you'll love another of his books, *Sing Me a Death Song*."

As the class period comes to a close, Tracy reminds students to concentrate on their revisions for papers. In addition, she shares a form for gathering book recommendations, a core piece for getting ready for the next phase of their workshop (see Figure 5.4), and encourages them to check with lots of folks they trust for suggestions. These book recommendations will provide a bridge to the upcoming choice unit.

Plans for Day Seven, Nonfiction Unit (day nine of the semester)	
Time	**Tasks**
12:05–12:25	Hand out cards for heterogeneous grouping. Microlessons: troublesome homophones, effective use of semicolons to support sentence variation and effect, use of dialogue/quotation marks.
12:25–1:15	Workshop time for writing, revising, editing.
1:15–1:35	Reading recommendations.
1:35–1:40	Reminders for next class.

Talk to your friends, relatives, teachers, etc., about books. Have at least three different people recommend a book for you to read. Aim for getting between five and ten book recommendations. Of course, you can get more if you want to!

Book Title	Author	Recommended By

Figure 5.4. Book Recommendations Sheet

Day Eight, Nonfiction Unit

Students grab their cards and settle in today with a hint of stress in the air. Papers are due soon! To get the creative juices flowing, Tracy introduces a quick writing invitation:

Writing Invitation 7

Go back in your notebooks to your initial list of writing possibilities. Look over the list quickly and select one special moment in your life that you remember with absolute clarity, one that you know you'll hold on to for years and years. Select that memory for a fastwrite using one of the following starts.

a. Open with dialogue (see the skills section of your notebook if you need a reminder).
b. Sensory details starting with the sense of smell.

Barry chooses an everyday event and kicks his writing off with dialogue:

"Damn Barry, this place is a pig sty!"

"Sorry Ma," I said, ashamed. I tried to avoid her eyes by looking at my holey socks. Bless those holey socks.

"What are you waiting for?" she asked sternly.

The Christmas lights were still up and it was the middle of March. Clothes were strewn and my dog sniffed the unfamiliar scents that covered a sweatshirt.

Thomas settles on a scene from his home, weaving in multiple sensory images:

As you walk down the shallow stairs you step off the soft carpet onto the cold cement. You travel past several rooms filled with clutter along a narrow path created by junk pushed to the side before entering into the small cubicle like room. Along the edges are several book cases and a dresser with a tv on top. As you walk in there is . . .

Groups buzz with quick observations about interesting words, stories, and settings.

The class today must embrace numerous activities. Most writers will engage in final editing and divide their time between gaining additional peer response—sometimes about a particular paragraph, a lead, or a sentence that doesn't seem to be working well, final editing—and drafting their self-evaluation letter to Tracy that will accompany the final draft. To support the self-evaluation, she provides the following directions.

Self-Evaluation Letter

Self-evaluation is essential to me as a writer because it helps me to reflect on my writing, come to a deeper understanding of it, and set future goals. I want you to go inside of your own writing, so you too can better understand yourself as a writer. I want you to write me a letter about your observations. You should use a standard letter format starting with "Dear Tracy." You will want to use paragraphs, vary your sentence structure, and let your voice come through. Brainstorm pieces of information that you can include in your letter.

Together, the class examines this prompt and brainstorms specific ideas about what might be helpful in such a letter. All students will complete an evaluation letter to accompany their final draft that is due at the next class. These letters allow students to share with Tracy some of the emotions that have gone into this type of research.

Students shift smoothly into these activities, and soon the buzz becomes soft whispers in isolated parts of the room. Today Linda is ready for another reader to provide fresh input into her "almost complete" draft. She takes her piece, now eight pages in length, to John. Together, they slowly make their way through "The Projects," looking carefully at sentence variation and word choice, and they make notes on the draft so that Linda will have them available as she moves back to her own work space to begin the process of final revision.

Over the past two days Zane's story about his grandfather has grown to six pages. He's already availed himself of a peer responder, and used those comments to do a careful revision on his final draft. He has time today to begin his evaluation letter for Tracy in which he reveals that he started out to investigate one aspect of family history only to find himself on an unpredictable path.

Students have learned to make every minute count, and they now have lots of practice in planning their own use of time. Some work to complete drafts, pausing to conference with themselves before plowing back into their revisions. Others use the remainder of the class time to seek response from peers or from Tracy. When Zane and others, whose drafts and self-evaluations are near completion, feel ready, they move directly into their self-selected nonfiction books. Self-directed reading time has been an increasingly significant part of the nonfiction unit and will be integral to the workshop for the remainder of the semester.

With minutes to go before the students leave, Tracy reminds them of the final preparations for the papers. There will be sharing at the next class, and she wants all the students to look forward to having an audience. Final drafts should come in along with all revision drafts and fastwrites that may have supported the development of the paper. In addition, the self-evaluation letter is a must.

Plans for Day Eight, Nonfiction Unit (day ten of the semester)	
Time	**Tasks**
12:05–12:25	Hand out cards for heterogeneous grouping. Fastwrite.
12:25–1:35	Workshop time for writing, revising, editing, letters of self-evaluation, choice reading.
1:35–1:40	Reminders for next class.

Day Nine, Nonfiction Unit

Today is filled with completion and transition activities as students seek final peer group response, make final revisions, and move into their reading of newly selected choice books. Together they brainstorm the kinds of feedback that would be most helpful from the peer response groups and then immediately move to them; each student will have the opportunity to read their work aloud to their writing partners. In addition, individual partners will have the opportunity to read each of the papers silently, taking time to write a response letter back to the author. The goal for this sharing is to help students learn more about what is effective in the papers and identify areas that may need clarification or elaboration.

Linda is ready for her peer response group. She has revised multiple times already, and she has incorporated response from John into the draft she shares today. With multiple responses, she will be able to see how various readers respond to things differently. The goal isn't to have others take over ownership of her writing; instead, by seeing multiple responses, she will be able to consider all comments and questions and make decisions about what—if anything—she will adjust in the piece at this stage. In addition, giving and receiving feedback allows her to both see techniques and special qualities in the writing of peers and to reinforce their use in her own writing.

Soon, with response in hand, Linda moves back to her own writing space, settles in to consider her feedback. Tracy takes this moment to add one more step in the process. "Writing," she says, "is never really finished. Even though this is a 'final' draft, go back into the text of the paper and mark it up one more time. Put on your best editing cap! What could be said more crisply, elaborated more strongly?"

The first page of Linda's final mark up of "The Projects" (see Figure 5.5) reflects her keen eye for details, wording, and word choice that she has developed over the past four weeks. She understands that every critical reading helps her tighten and sharpen the focus of the writing, a sophisticated skill supported

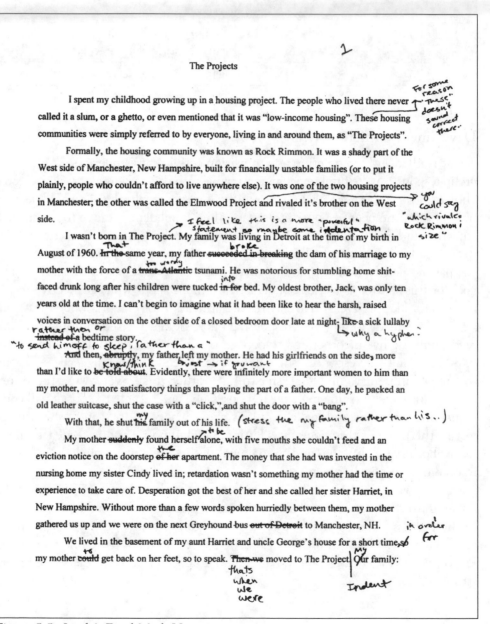

Figure 5.5. Linda's Final Mark Up

by reading well-written texts, discussing author's craft, and supported practice, practice, practice.

She has worked hard on her writing, and her effort and dedication to the work comes through clearly in her Dear Tracy self-evaluation letter (see Figure 5.6). She is proud of this nonfiction narrative, and she has a right to be! She's followed

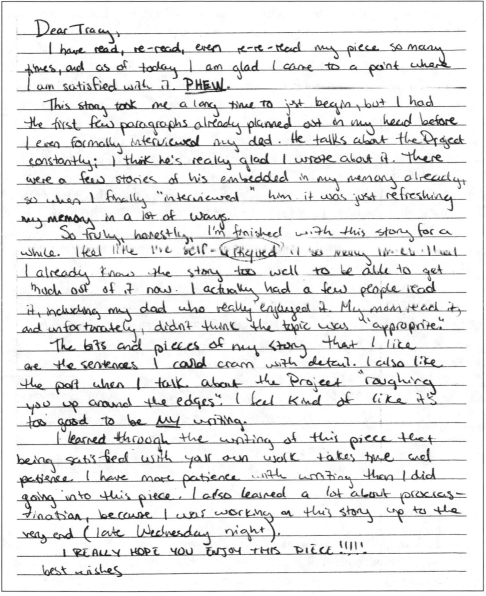

Figure 5.6. Linda's Self-Evaluation Letter

a real story, completed primary and secondary research, and crafted a narrative that holds the attention of the reader. Moreover, she has not only developed skill in writing, she has developed the ability to reflect on the quality of her own words and mold them into sentences and phrases that are exceptional—that seem "too good to be *my* writing."

Zane finished his evaluation letter at the previous class. Today, he shares his paper with a peer response group, carefully collecting responses for further consideration. He then moves to his writing space and, like Linda, looks over his feedback and does a final mark up of his paper for himself. Figure 5.7 illustrates the critical eye he applies to his final draft as he considers possibilities for tightening the prose, for clarifying or elaborating a passage. Page two of this marked up draft sharply demonstrates how Zane has grown in his ability to develop a piece and how his sense of sentence and passage development has grown in sophistication.

As students prepare papers for submission, they create a portfolio representing all the drafts that led to the final paper. For some students, this includes four to five full drafts in addition to the final one, a self-evaluation letter, peer response letters, and a skills sheet in which they recorded specific skills that they targeted for work during the unit. They carry the bundles with them to the Round Table that ends the week where, once again, they offer one another thanks and apologies and they celebrate the completion of a major project that represents significant, thoughtful work.

Plans for Day Nine, Nonfiction Unit (day eleven of the semester)	
Time	**Tasks**
1:35–2:15	Peer response groups. Individual final mark up. Completion of self-evaluation letters. Completion of skills sheet.
2:15–2:30	Round Table for thanks and apologies.

Taking a Step Back

As we look across the three weeks devoted to the introductory study of nonfiction, it seems remarkable how much instruction has been woven into such a limited amount of time. Not only have students become acquainted with numerous genres of nonfiction, they have also had rich opportunities to develop their own

[Other's voice] ~~father's voice.~~ Bill's father cleared his throat and began his tale.

" Back when I was just a kid, about the age you are now, Tom, I was invited on a hunting trip with *[the men of the family's]* my father, grandfather, older brothers, and uncles. This was back in Denmark, mind you. We went to a forest that was ~~about~~ a three day walk from our house and set up camp. I was having the time of my life; the men of the family were starting to accept me into the fold. This would be my first steps on the path of manhood."

" We went through two days without any trouble; my father and uncle both killed a deer apiece. Normally that would have been enough, but my father said that we couldn't go home without me ~~killing~~ *[having killed]* my first animal, be it rabbit, *[a]* squirrel, *[an]* or elephant. Wanting to prove myself, I went out the next day with a vengeance. I tried to use everything I had been taught, techniques passed down from generation to generation. I tried hard, too hard. I got real tense ~~and nervous~~ and jumpy. I would whirl around, looking for the ~~slightest cause of~~ *[cause of the slightest]* noise. I wanted more than anything to prove myself, to finally be taken seriously. I was so blinded by my desire, I shot and killed my own father."

At this, Bill's jaw dropped. He was dumbfounded. The man he idolized, the man that could do no wrong, had just admitted to one of the worst wrongs you could possibly commit. *[He looked quietly at his brothers and sister.]* Had ~~he~~ *[they]* heard ~~his~~ *[their]* father correctly?

[They] ~~He~~ leaned closer.

"Of all the things that could have possibly happened, this was by far the worst. ~~My grandfather almost killed me on the spot.~~ *[The men]* ~~They~~ were beyond furious. I had committed one of the single most heinous acts a man could commit. And through all of this, I simply could not believe what had happened. I had actually killed my own father."

"*[I]* ~~t~~was even worse when we returned home. My mother ~~completely broke~~ *[was utterly broken]*. She could not

Figure 5.7. Zane's Final Mark Up

writing while engaged in primary and secondary research. First introducing various skills and craft lessons within the context of meaningful reading and writing, Tracy has orchestrated both cyclical reminders of the skills and their transfer into student writing through frequent mini- and microlessons. She has chosen to focus on a narrow band of skills during this study, ones that she identified as important from her analysis of student fastwrites. By keeping the focus tight, she has avoided the problems of a curriculum that is a "mile wide and an inch deep," the kind of coverage that tends to lead to shallow learning that is less likely to be of use in the future.

By this point, the notion of nonfiction has been opened up substantially for these students. As will be discussed later, many came into the class with a prejudice against nonfiction, reacting to essays as the dominant (and unappreciated) genre for high school. Now, they not only know of many other nonfiction genres through which they might choose to shape a message, they also understand that quality nonfiction writing requires as great an investment as does fiction—a fact that had eluded them previously.

A transparent goal for this unit has been the shifting of responsibility for writing to the student and away from the teacher, and as anyone who has taught high school knows, such a shift does not happen by chance. Tracy has woven a tight fabric, carefully articulating and institutionalizing routines and systems that support students working independently and help her to maintain a high level of organization. Significantly, systems are set up to support the authors' work. Students learn to manage both time and process—from writing groups, to peer response groups, to conferences with themselves, to writer's notebooks—with one goal in mind: to improve their writing. Everything in this class is channeled to that same goal.

Continuous attention to community building has supported the development of a collective sense of responsibility. Consistent opportunities for writing, sharing, whole and small group discussion, getting and receiving feedback, and moving back to one's own space for work have established productive and predictable structures to support young writers as they grow in their craft, become more self-reliant, and assume greater personal responsibility.

Certainly, having choice in topic and nonfiction genre is a significant contributor in building student ownership for their writing. While gathering information and composing, students have had opportunities to engage others in their fact finding and as responders/contributors to their emerging drafts; to share and discuss their writing with peers, one-on-one and in small groups; to hold conferences with themselves as practice for looking at their own work as a reader and writer; to mark up their drafts in the same way a professional editor might do; and to make choices about how to use the feedback and information they received. Exercising personal choice and initiative throughout the writing has resulted in strong commitment to the final pieces that were shared in class and, in numerous cases, with individuals beyond the school.

Self-reliance has led to a heightened sense of power. These students understand that it is the province of the writer to make decisions about her writing.

Building on multiple opportunities to identify and discuss excellent features of good writing, students have developed an internalized sense of interesting sentence flow and effective use of punctuation; they understand the punch that dialogue or crisp details can provide. Of course, these lessons will be built on across the semester, but final nonfiction papers already show evidence of the use of the techniques and skills Tracy has chosen to emphasize for their work thus far.

Self-reliance and power are tightly bound to reflection. In a myriad of ways, Tracy has fashioned the instructional environment to increase her students' reflective abilities. From considering their role—both their rights and responsibilities—within a democratic workshop environment to writing reflective self-assessments, students have experienced rich opportunities to take a step back, to think, and to make judgments based on evaluation.

At the core of successful writing is having something to say . . . having an investment in the message that will be sent into the world. The nonfiction pieces generated by the students reflect their interest and commitment to their words. Both contribute significantly to the growth of students' writing identities and to the development of their writing skills.

Part 3

• • • • • •

Teaching Through Self-Selected Reading
and Writing Experiences

As students move from their intensive focus on nonfiction into a series of weeks during which they assume more choice over their reading and writing experiences, they will build on the processes and systems that are already in place in the rich community of the classroom. Tracy has developed a high level of expectation for her students, and in most cases, the students themselves have embraced these standards. She will continue to push their growth forward through frequent writing invitations and periodic skills and craft lessons. She also understands that writers do not write in a vacuum; because of this, students will be surrounded by rich resources to challenge their thinking and support their development of texts.

The ground has been laid for the transition to the openness of the new unit already, with students seeking suggestions from trusted others beyond the classroom for books that comprise their "must read" list of recommendations. These lists will continue to grow through the remainder of the semester, and offering ample possibilities to whet reading appetites—their own and those of peers.

Many students have discovered a new interest in nonfiction as a result of their first unit. Some, like Celly, will take this interest into their free-choice writing unit. Others, like Abby, will gravitate back to familiar genres, seeking to deepen their competence with narrative fiction. Still others, like Barry, will strike out for a completely new genre for writing, in his case developing a portfolio of poetry.

Throughout the next three weeks, the writers' notebooks will provide invaluable support as students reflect on previous skills and craft lessons, revisit earlier writing ideas, and continue to add to each; in addition, the notebook will hold new possibilities as students launch into new writing invitations. Through the next three chapters, we'll take a close look at the ways in which Tracy infuses essential instruction based on continued analysis of student work. We'll note the ways in which she continues to urge students to move forward as they take on more responsibility for their own writing and reading. Finally, through the work of three representative students, Barry, Abby, and Celly, we'll observe the ways all of this comes together as students develop pieces of writing for which they have both pride and commitment.

6

Claiming Power

Day One, Choice Unit

"What do you want to write?" Tracy asks as students settle in for class. "Where do we get ideas for our writing?"

With little prompting, possibilities fill the air: things that we wonder about; stories that let us build from our imaginations; new types of writing that we haven't tried before; things from our own lives and experiences.

"If you could write anything you wanted to write, what would that be? What piece of writing would be significant to you?" The question is followed by a brief pause, as students ponder the options they have before them. They are excited today because they've been looking forward to the opportunity for more self-directed work. Today's class reaffirms and builds on the systems already in place that will help them negotiate this new habitable space to their best advantage as they continue to grow as readers and writers and also accept continued responsibility for supporting the progress of their peers.

Three management tools will be important in particular. Earlier, Tracy opened up the conversation about book recommendations and provided each student with a recommendation sheet on which to collect titles of outstanding pieces of literature and names of favorite authors. Already Zane has collected seven titles from peers and one from an outside source (see Figure 6.1). In small groups, students quickly share snippets of books they have begun to explore before moving to a very quick round-the-room sharing of the most highly recommended titles. This is a time for cross-pollination, as students capture new possibilities for reading. Each student's list of recommendations goes into the writer's notebook for ready reference.

In addition to in-class time for reading and writing, students are expected to devote as much time as possible to these activities outside of class. A second tool,

Book Recommendations

Talk to your friends, relatives, teachers, etc., about books. Have at least three
different people recommend a book for you to read. Aim for getting between five
and ten book recommendations. Of course, you can get more if you want to!

Book Title	Author	Recommended by...
Star girl	Jerry Spinelli	Lauren
Perks of being a Wallflower	Stephen Chobolski	~~Lauren~~ Alia
Bachman Books	Stephen King	Lauren
A child called it	David Pelzer	Alia
Prozac Nation	Elizabeth Wurtzel	Alia
Now, more, and again		
I know that much is true		Maggie Kben

Figure 6.1. Zane's Book Recommendations

Writing Workshop

For the next ten days, we are going to do a little experiment. I want you to dedicate time every day to reading and writing that is meaningful to you. I want you to breathe the life of a reader and writer. Please use this sheet to keep track of the work that you are doing and when you are doing it. On March 22, you will turn in this sheet along with your out of class writing.

	Reading Time	Reading Pages	Writing Time	Writing Topic/Genre
Saturday, March 12	20 min.	random books @ library	10 min.	• non-fiction writing paper started
Sunday, March 13	20 min.	magazines for fun	—	—
Monday, March 14	—	—	45 min.	• non-fiction writing • random thoughts
Tuesday, March 15	30 min.	16 pgs. of Reading Lolita in Tehran	20 min.	• diary-like • random thoughts
Wednesday, March 16	40-45 min.	31 pgs. of Interpreter of maladies	30 min.	• choice writing started.
Thursday, March 17	30 min	15 pgs. of I.O.M.	↓	↓
Friday, March 18	30 min.	29 pgs. of I.O.M.	20 min.	• a letter
Saturday, March 19	—	—	—	—
Sunday, March 20	20 min.	13 pgs. of I.O.M.	1 hour	• choice writing • non-fiction
Monday, March 21	15 min.	17 pgs. of I.O.M.	1 hour	"

Figure 6.2. Celly's Personal Workshop Record

the Writing Workshop Record (see Figure 6.2), helps students manage their time by tracking their reading and writing outside of class. Celly's Writing Workshop Record illustrates how, over a two-week period, she ventures into a variety of genres for writing and how her reading includes a smorgasbord of books in addition to magazines and a particular title that she works on over time. In conversations with Tracy, she is encouraged to think about the diverse ways she uses reading and writing for both school and authentic life purposes.

Finally, each student is reminded to maintain a Skills Sheet Record (see Figure 6.3) to keep track of the types of skills they focus on as they move through their written pieces. In Figure 6.3, we see that Linda focuses on three skills on a particular day. Maintaining this type of daily record helps to keep the skills visible for the student, helps Tracy track each student's specific skill development, and, once again, reinforces the fact that students are expected to take ownership and responsibility for their own learning.

Once these housekeeping tasks are addressed, Tracy asks students to open their writer's notebooks. They will do two things quickly to encourage fluency.

Skills Sheet

for _____

Date addressed	Skill(s)	Date mastered
3/17	Shortening sentences to create more dramatic effect (condense ideas)	
3/17	Use of apostropes for possessive nouns, etc.	
3/17	Use of semi-colons (approprite placing)	

Figure 6.3. Linda's Skills Sheet

One at a time, Tracy places three poems on the overhead projector—"Owl Pellets" by Ralph Fletcher, and "If I Were a Poem" and "Chicks Up Front," both by Sara Holbrook—and asks students to write as quickly as they can in response to each.

Owl Pellets

A month ago
in biology lab
you sat close to me
knee touching mine
your sweet smell
almost drowning out
the formaldehyde stink
which crinkled up
your nose
while I dissected
our fetal pig.

Now I take apart
this owl pellet
small bag that holds
skin and hair and bones
little skeletons
what the owl ate
but couldn't digest
and coughed back up.
You sit with Jon Fox
ignore me completely
laugh at his dumb jokes
let your head fall onto
his bony shoulder
while I attempt
to piece together
with trembling hands
the tiny bones
of a baby snake.

Certain things
are just about
impossible
to swallow.

—Ralph Fletcher, from *I Am Wings: Poems About Love*

Chicks Up Front

Before and After, we stand separate,
Stuck to the same beer-soaked floor,
fragranced, facing the same restroom mirror.
Adjusting loose hairs—mine brown, hers purple.
Fumbling for lipstick—mine pink, hers black—
a color I couldn't wear anyway since the convention of lines
gathered around my mouth about a year ago, won't leave.
We avoid eye contact; both of us are afraid of being carded.

Mature, I suppose I should speak, but what can I say
to the kind of hostility that turns hair purple and lips black?
Excuse me, I know I never pierced my nose,
But hey, I was revolting once, too.
Back . . . before I joined the PTA,
when Wonder Bras meant, "where'd I put that."
I rebelled against the government system,
the male-female system, the corporate system, you name it.
I marched, I changed, I demonstrated,
And when shit got passed around,
I was there, sweetheart, and I inhaled.
Does she know that tear gas
makes your nose run worse than your eyes?
Would she believe that I was a volunteer
when they called "chicks up front"?
Because no matter what kind of hand-to-hand combat
the helmeted authoritarians may have been engaged in at home,
they were still hesitant to hit girls with batons in the streets.
"CHICKS UP FRONT!"
And we marched, and we marched,
and we marched right back home:
Where we bore the children
we were not going to bring into this mad world,
and we brought them home to houses
we were never going to wallpaper in those Laura Ashley prints,
and we joined the corporate mongers
we were not going to let supervise our lives,
where we skyrocketed to middle-management positions
accepting less money than
we were never going to take anyway
and spending it on the Barbie Dolls
we were not going to buy for our daughters.

And after each party for our comings and goings,
we whisked the leftovers into dust pans,

90

debriefing and talking each other down from the drugs
and the men as if they were different.
Resuscitating one another as women do,
mouth to mouth.
That some of those who we put up front
really did get beaten down and others now bathe
themselves daily in Prozac to maintain former freshness.
Should I explain what tedious work it is putting role models together
and how sometimes strategic pieces get sucked up by this vacuum?
And while we intended to take one giant leap for womankind,
I wound up taking one small step, alone.

What can I say
At that moment our eyes meet in the mirror,
which they will.
What can I say to purple hair, black lips and a nose ring?
What can I say?
"Take care."

—Sara Holbrook, from *Chicks Up Front*

If I Were a Poem
If I were a poem,
I would grab you by the ankles
And rustle you up to your every leaf.
I would gather your branches
in the power of my winds and pull you skyward,
if I were a poem.

If I were a poem,
I would walk you down beside the rushing stream,
swollen with spring, put thunder in your heart,
then lay you down, a new lamb, to sing you softly to sleep,
if I were a poem.

If I were a poem,
I wouldn't just talk to you of politics, society and change,
I would be a raging bonfire to strip you of your outer wrap,
and then I would reach within and with one touch
ignite the song in your own soul.

If I were a poem,
I would hold my lips one breath away from yours
and inflate you with such desire as can exist
only just out of reach, and then I would move
the breadth of one bee closer not to sting,
but to brush you with my wings as I retreat

to leave you holding nothing but a hungry, solitary sigh,
if I were a poem.

If I were a poem,
my thoughts would finally be put to words
through your own poetry, I would push you that far,
if I were a poem.

—Sara Holbrook, from *Chicks Up Front*

In small groups students share their names and fastwrites before a few, like Abby, share with the class (see Figure 6.4). Abby's responses take her thoughts in widely varying directions: a childhood memory; a playful, if satirical, reaction; an identification of the serious, though different, battles young women fight today. Linda's responses initially take her to an outpouring of an emotional memory; then to a poem that responds to "Chicks Up Front" by entering into the poem and thinking through a character in it; and finally a haunting image of an empty body, a full soul, and the emotions that dangle between (see Figure 6.5). Quick responses wake up the

---

Response 1
Certain things are just about impossible to swallow. This reminds me of things that you can swallow but shouldn't. My best friend when I was little was named Brianna. One day she was at our house and my mom had a bowl of Jolly Ranchers. Brianna was eating one, jumping, then choking. My mom gave her the Heimlich maneuver. (response to "Owl Pellets")

Response 2
If I were a poem I'd mock your poem.
Repeating over and over
The same phrase, then
Casting you into the swelling stream
To see if the lightning in your heart
Mixes maliciously. (response to "If I Were a Poem")

Response 3
Chick's up front. In our segregation we have different battles. We hate our own image. Women, young women today have new battles. We must stand up to a media that says we're materialistic objects for sex. Put on your clothes. Don't let men throw money at your naked body. Respect is something you must first have yourself before you can get it from others. (response to "Chicks Up Front")

Figure 6.4. Abby's Fastwrite Response to Poems

writer's imagination with responses to sharp images, rich language, interesting technique, and they offer a great way to get writing flowing.

"Where else can we get ideas for writing?" Tracy asks. "Don't forget the writing possibilities from the beginning of the semester!" Students rummage through their writer's notebooks to retrieve the lists they did during that first week. With a quick glance, Abby sees that she has over fifty ideas for writing (see Figure 6.6)—including

---

Response 1
Certain things are just about impossible to swallow, like the lump in your throat when you can't find the right words to say so the wrong ones spill out of your mouth, then clumsily onto the floor. When you try to stop crying and your breaths are short little gasps, the feeling overpowers you and . . .

Response 2
Happiness, content, warm, fuzzy
just out of reach
conflicts, heartbreak, its wispy veil
dangles delicately between
an empty body and a
whole full soul
like an out of body experience
hallucinations.

Response 3
I stand in the dirty bathroom
casually neglecting the obscene graffiti
and messy joints masquerading as squares
looking into the mirror
I see a girl, with purple hair
alongside a woman. A woman,
just an ordinary woman
applying pink lipstick to an aged mouth
and I wonder
does she assume that I've got ambitions?
When she lowers her eyes
is she afraid to accidentally see
condoms? Or a secret hidden behind by
blackened lips?

Figure 6.5. Linda's Fastwrite Response to Poems

Writing possibilities–
 assignment #1

10 of the best things ever to happen to me:
1. I moved to ann arbor from Dexter.
2. I got into community.
3. I started dating Roland.
4. I got my liscense and my car.
5. I joined the pioneer swim team.
6. I got into my choice art school.
7. I went to pre-college at Pratt.
8. My mom's tumor was found to be benine.
9. When I learned to read
10. I moved into my sweet house.

10 of the worst things ever to happen to me:
1. I had to give up my dog & cat when my mom remarried.
2. my mom was diagnosed with cancer.
3. My uncle screwed my mom out of our bussiness
4. My dog died while I was at camp
5. My aunt died of breast cancer
6. I had to go to Forsythe middle school.
7. My former-best friend Jacque broke up our friendship
8. I was forced into christianity
9. I became bulemic in middle school (I'm better don't worry)
10. I realized my dad was full of shit

10 things I'm proud of:
1. getting accepted into art school.
2. My puppy Dugann, and my dog Monty
3. My new painting
4. My music tastes
5. My Friends
6. My knoledge of rocks & minerals, and their properties
7. My mom
8. My extensive book and comic collection

Figure 6.6. Abby's Writing Possibilities

9. My School
10. My Appearance

10 moments with family or friends:
1. going to the hotsprings in Japan with roland and his family
2. playing with cedric
3. smoking in the arb with spelmo and ryan
4. chicago trip with jacque
5. hookah bar in East village on last night of art school.
6. Moving mattresses with allison
7. back drawing with my mom when I was little
8. talking with my brother while he smoked out a window in france.
9. Hiking up to Machu Pitchu with my mom and step dad
10. My first first puppy playtime with Becca.

10 learning experiences (life or school):
1. applying to college
2. failing a community tradition
3. my mom's illness
4. my transition into community
5. paying for the dammages of my first car accident
6. Almost drowning in the brighton band and being saved
7. when my gerbil got out and when we caught him bec bt me
8. middle school
9. getting lost in Brooklyn NY
10. loosing my best friend

Figure 6.6. *Continued*

one that deals with body image for girls, a topic that surfaced in her fastwrite response (Figure 6.4) and one for which she certainly has strong feelings. There's no shortage of topics to consider.

As students move into their extended block for individual reading and writing, there's a bit of shifting around the room. Some move to the computers, others back to the book stacks. Tracy moves from desk to desk, her State of the Class sheets in hand. She structures her data gathering sheets to meet her unique needs, using one sheet for each student to track each individual's progress, ultimately copying the reporting sheet for each student as a type of progress report. There are fifty minutes devoted to workshop today, which gives Tracy sufficient time to meet with each student briefly and check in on their progress.

With ten minutes to go, students move out of individual work to ask questions, share a "gem" from their reading, or offer a snippet from the writing they've done today. The quick sharing session allows them to leave the room with a sense of the work that is under way and rich language ringing in their ears.

Plans for Day One, Choice Unit (day twelve of the semester)

Time	Tasks
12:05–12:20	Reviewing tools for the unit.
12:20–12:35	Responses to prompts.
12:35–12:40	Revisiting writing possibilities.
12:40–1:30	Reading and writing workshop time.
1:30–1:40	Closing share.

Day Two, Choice Unit

To the students' surprise, today's class starts with sharing from a visitor—me! I've been working all semester on a piece of writing that I'm excited about, one that I've revised a dozen times already. Between this class and the last one, I intended to give the piece one last review before mailing it off. As I'd read the piece aloud at home, walking up and down my hallway, listening to every word with a pen in hand, I'd found myself stopping often to make notes, draw arrows, substitute a word, and even restructure the order of a few paragraphs.

The sample I share with the students today reflects a substantial revision over the previous draft, changes that will make the piece much stronger and tighter. To think I had believed the piece was finished! Tracy and I use this real-life illustration to move the students into two short minilessons, the first to encourage their recognition of strong writing and the second to hone their revision skills.

Tracy has collected samples of strong writing from the recently completed nonfiction papers. She starts with four excerpts, asking students to read them silently from the overhead screen and to respond, in their writer's notebooks, with observations about the writing.

Excerpt 1

She didn't bother to wipe them (tears). She stood still while the tears ran down her cheeks. She couldn't move. Others around her were clapping and shouting, but Karen stood still. And listened. She listened until King ended his speech, and the entire crowd erupted into an explosion of applause and shouting and praise. Karen looked around her and caught Nathan's eye. He had been crying too. She took his hand, once again, and squeezed it tightly. And she smiled. (VK)

Excerpt 1

"Stand up straight now, Mary, I need to measure you." Carolyn, my older's sister's cold fingers slid down my back as she pulled the tape measurer about me. "What's this?" she said as she lifted the back of my shirt up, "Your back, it looks all crooked."

"What?" I twisted around trying to see my back, "What'd you mean it's crooked?"

"Well, look at it! Never mind," she said, seeing me twisting around, "don't hurt yourself now."

When Carolyn had finished getting my measurements for my jumper, I tried to see my back in the mirror. I stared at it. Was it bad if it wasn't straight? As I helped my mom with the dishes that night, I asked her about my back.

"Carolyn says my back isn't straight, mama." I stacked bowls in the cupboard. "What's that mean? Is it something bad?"

"It's probably nothing. I'll take a look at it after I clean up," she said waving me away. (LB)

Excerpt 3

Don stared at me directly. His stare was like having burning knives stuck into my eyes. He said, "Lieutenant, I should court marshal you right back to the States where you belong if you choose to defy your position in this army. But you're too important to this squadron, and we need you to remain here. But, believe me, if I could I would discharge you right now." (JK)

Excerpt 4

I lay in bed, covers pulled up and windows shut. Despite these precautions, shouts and distant, undetermined bangs rang in my ears, like an unrecognizable tune that's increasing in volume. A single, solitary tear strolled down my cheek and tumbled, like a miniature flood, onto the mattress. There it immersed itself among fibers and threads, until it melted away into a dark blotch that would have been my paradise. I stared at it in sudden confusion, not knowing what to make of this new occurrence. The noises grew louder. (CD)

What made the excerpts strong? Students note the varied sentence structure, the way an author puts the reader directly into the piece, and the use of dialogue to add punch and interest.

Tracy places five more samples on the screen for their review.

Excerpt 5

Back then, our parents were too caught up in the strings that making minimum wage had tied to them, turning them into puppets with narrow-minded goals of earning enough to keep up residence in the Project. There was a forced carelessness about our moms and dads. They were faced with the dilemma of providing economically or providing parentally. Making money or making memories. In the end, society and "the real world" bit them in the ass and convinced them that their children would be much more secure living in a household lacking a parental figure rather than in an alley instilled with strong Christian values. It was inevitable that they had to work while we were left to our own devices. (LK)

Excerpt 6

The wind blew across the dry fields, sending clouds of dust swirling through the grove of pecan trees growing next to the small farmhouse. A loose shutter broke its bonds and slapped against the house. Several dogs sought shelter from the stinging dust by wriggling under the porch. From the windows came the warm glow of oil lamps lighting a dinner table. (ZS)

Excerpt 7

The remote dropped out of my hands as it fell limply against my side. My heart beat faster as the cup of coffee was forgotten and getting cold. The scene in front of me was something like out of the movies. The familiar twin towers of New York crumbling like they were made out of sand, people the size of ants jumping without a second thought out of burning buildings, the planes slicing through them like scissors through paper; it looked so unnatural. (CL)

Excerpt 8

Wasilla looked in the mirror at her own reflection. It had been so long since she had looked at herself in the mirror. Her eyes were dark and swollen from restless nights. Her lips were cracked and dry. Her complexion was pale and hollow as a ghost. She had lost all the life within her. She had started off as a young girl, and now she had become a woman. Her mind veered toward the past. She shut her eyes, as she tried to restrain the images that she wanted to forget. In her mind, she was younger. She was a little girl, and stood in front of her house, giggling, as her father played around with her. He held her hands and swung her around in circles, faster and faster. (AM)

Excerpt 9

I knew my father had finished his story. Just how he sat there with a crumble filled plate laid in front of him and how he didn't say another word. He just looked through the glass back door. Looking outside. At what I don't know . . . Also, it was the look on his face. I would never forget it. Thick with memories. It didn't seem like it would be right to pull him out of the world where things were simple and wide-eyed, so I left him there in his thoughts. I owed it to him. (AH)

"What do you observe now?" Tracy asks. This time the thinking and observing go a bit deeper. Students recognize the effective use of

- fragments for particular impact
- imagery and metaphor
- techniques such as explode a moment and snapshot
- words used in unconventional ways
- dialogue—sometimes in a cropped fashion for special effect
- varying paragraph lengths to build interest
- personification
- techniques such as manipulation of stance or time—author immediately putting readers inside the place, story, or character's mind

With these observations captured on an overhead transparency, Tracy offers up the second surprise for the day: students receive back their own nonfiction papers, but without a grade included. Instead, Tracy has provided a few comments and now asks students once again—with fresh eyes—to review and revise their papers, marking them up as they've done in the past, as a professional editor might do. She very briefly reviews the editing notations they have in the skills section of the writer's notebooks to support this process.

There are a few groans around the room. Students are invited to revisit these papers anytime during the hour; some tackle the task immediately so they won't have to interrupt their reading and writing time later. Others, anxious to get into their new writing, put off their review until the end of class or negotiate taking the papers home to work on later. The task isn't intended to be an arduous one, just an opportunity to see how our eyes sharpen when we step back from a piece of writing and revisit it anew.

Once again Tracy moves around the class softly, capturing data for her State of the Class Record. Several students have asked for a moment to confer on a topic or question, and she makes a point of getting to them first. As described earlier, this class has a diverse student population, with about one-third of the students dealing with some type of learning difficulty. The workshop gives Tracy the essential time to check in with these students, to further explain concepts, to more directly coach their reading and writing, and to connect them to extra support if needed. If there are other professionals available to work with a student, this provides a safe time for providing that instructional support or for allowing opportunities for peer coaching within the classroom.

As she moves about the class, Tracy finds that several students have questions about spelling, a topic for which she has invested lots of time and interest. With ten minutes to go, she pulls the class back together for a final microlesson: the introduction of two quick spelling strategies. First, she reminds students of the wisdom of using a special section in their writer's notebook to record high-frequency problem words—those words they use all the time but tend to struggle with each time. Having ready access will make the use of these words more efficient, and repeated exposure to correct spelling also increases the likelihood of remembering troublesome words. Second, she describes a common visual strategy, have-a-go, which encourages writing a problematic word as many ways as the student thinks it might be spelled before analyzing the possibilities to determine the correct spelling, a popular strategy for enhancing visual discrimination.

For example, two words pop up today: probably and definitely.

probably	deffinently
probablee	definetly
probabley	definitly
probaly	definently
	definitely

When writing words in this way, the correct spelling often jumps out, making it easier to identify which one is right. In earlier lessons Tracy has shared other ideas to support spelling growth including strategies for creating mnemonic devices that help with recall of troublesome words. She encourages students to draw on strategies they have learned to help master these two words, and to also add these words to their personal dictionaries.

Plans for Day Two, Choice Unit (day thirteen of the semester)	
Time	**Tasks**
12:05–12:30	Minilessons: revision of a final draft; quick review of editing notes. Minilesson: observing strong writing features.
12:30–1:25	Reading and writing workshop time.
1:25–1:35	Microlesson on spelling.
1:35–1:40	Closing share.

Day Three, Choice Unit

With the end of the first week at hand, many students have multiple pieces of writing started and waiting in their writer's notebooks. Tracy begins class today with a short microskills lesson on the use of *then* and *than*, resulting from her review of their most recent fastwrites and a craft lesson on leads.

Use of **Then** and **Than**
Remember! *Than* is a comparison. Think of a mnemonic such as comparing an apple with an artichoke. Let the *an* before both help you remember the *an* in *than*.

Then is an adverb that tells *when*. Remember *then/when* to help you remember how to use *then* correctly.

Short skills reminders such as this take less than two minutes. With a reminder to use *then* and *than* correctly in writing today, students are provided immediate reinforcement; because the skill is noted in writer's notebooks and will be referenced periodically during the semester, it will be one that is readily available, increasing the likelihood of mastery.

Students have talked about leads before, but today's lesson directly addresses four ways to craft interesting leads.

Crafting Interesting Leads
Authors commonly use one these four types of leads.

- *Big Potato Leads:* Jump into the middle of your story, and leave the reader wanting more.
- *Snapshot Leads:* Create a picture in the reader's mind.
- *Talking Leads:* Start with dialogue.
- *Thinking Leads:* Start with a thought inside a character or within yourself.

Tracy encourages students to take a quick look at the book they are reading and asks, "How did the author start? Does the type of lead the author used fit into one of these categories? If not, how would you describe the lead the author used?" Students check out their books and volunteers share examples of each of the four types, giving Tracy the opportunity to encourage sharing not only of techniques for opening a longer story, but of the various books as well.

Similarly, the writing invitation for today takes little time, but pays off with a big return in the future work as students grapple with *showing* through descriptive details instead of *telling*, thus helping the reader to visualize.

Writing Invitation 8
Think of a place that you know very well. Write as much as you can with the goal of putting the reader inside of that place without mentioning it by name. You can include characters, dialogue, and/or other sensory details. Your focus is on creating a place, not a story.

Students spend about ten minutes with their descriptive writing, attempting to also use one of the types of leads introduced above and to weave in a correct use of *then* and *than*. Here are some examples of the writing they produce.

I counted 10 cans and 5 bottles on the dust-ridden table. Sitting to the side, an ashtray overflowed and something sticky had been spilled, not cleaned up. Ploping down on a broken grey sofa the pleasant stench of stale beer and cigarettes wafted up to meet me. Gag!

Allison wanders in from the other room. She gazes blankly at the new poorly applied orange wall paint, kicks over an empty beer can as she sits down, and *then* gives me a look that plainly says, "why the hell did you bring Nick?" (Abby)

"It's comfy," I looked around at the cold bare walls, in awe by my surroundings.

She let out a little laugh. "Yea, as comfy as it can get . . ."

I smiled and looked at her pleasantly. The room was coated in the stench of plastic and Clorox. The sheets were colored in an ugly beige, which made my insides melt. I felt tense and cluttered.

The wires strung from her wrists made me uneasy. I sat in my chair in the corner of the room, gripping and scratching on the wood beneath my nails. I looked at her, now appearing less angelic and more undesirable.

I would rather have been outside *than* nauseated by what was around me. I felt as if I were being suffocated. *Then*, she looked at me contentedly. "I'm sorry . . ." (Allison)

Sharing again fills the air with interesting story snippets. As with all other writing, these pieces are dated and stored in writer's notebooks.

Because today is the short class for the week, workshop time is abbreviated; Tracy quickly checks on students' writing and reading contracts before pulling the class back together for closing thanks and apologies.

Plans for Day Three, Choice Unit (day fourteen of the semester)	
Time	**Tasks**
1:30–1:40	Skills lesson on *then* and *than*. Craft lesson on leads.
1:40–1:55	Writing Invitation 8—showing not telling. Sharing of fastwrites.
1:55–2:20	Workshop time.
2:20–2:30	Thanks and apologies.

Taking a Step Back

The move into greater student autonomy within the choice unit builds seamlessly on the systems Tracy has structured over the previous three weeks. Nothing is lost in translation! Tools like short micro- and minilessons to reinforce skills and craft, the writer's notebook, and frequent fastwrites coupled with small and/or whole group sharing have been institutionalized. Not only do students understand these tools, they expect them.

As has been noted earlier, high school students come to the workshop classroom with a long history of school experiences. While most students embrace the opportunity to spend blocks of time developing writing they choose, some find the openness of the writing time a bit bewildering—at least at first. For these students, choice is harder and the need for more coaching is evident. The operational systems that Tracy has established provide the time for her to work directly with students who need greater support and guidance.

As with earlier classes, there is one pervasive goal in the free-choice unit: to grow as writers. Early in the semester, students created lists of writing possibilities. These possibilities, the books they read, and the literature pieces provided for response by Tracy continuously provide ideas and models that invite writing. The workshop affords blocks of time for reading and writing, but the high school day—even with a block schedule—just doesn't offer enough minutes for all the reading and writing students need to do. To help encourage and track the outside-of-class connection, students maintain Book Recommendations Sheets (see Figure 5.4) and Writing Workshop Records (see Appendix B), effectively knitting together the continuous encouragement to read and write at home with the expectation to do so at school.

The Book Recommendations log helps to make book sharing a community affair. Many adult readers describe how important it is to share a good book once they have finished reading it. Through a process of going beyond the classroom to trusted adults and peers and then taking time to share recommendations with classmates, the pool of interesting literature becomes rich and extensive. Students have learned to trust each other, and the enthusiasm that is evident as one after the other shares a juicy book is the best possible recommendation for others.

The personal workshop records help students to remain aware of the time and effort they are investing in reading and writing. Being accountable for tracking their own work builds personal responsibility and ownership.

Though students assume more and more control of their time during the choice unit, instruction continues. Through ongoing skills and craft lessons, Tracy continues to address student writing needs that she identifies by analyzing their work or from short individual conferences. These lessons are personally relevant and specific; each lesson is immediately put to use in new pieces of writing and also stored in the writer's notebooks for future use, a handy source for help and reinforcement as needs crop up during the semester. High schools students often need to hear the same thing many times before they own the information. In the workshop, Tracy takes every opportunity to pick up the threads of earlier lessons and apply them to new applications.

Through frequent modeling students recognize that writing is very much a recursive process. Even writing that is thought to be "finished" may be taken to a new level when read later with fresh eyes, an observation that was completely new to some students. Adult modeling is important to this process, but just as effective is returning student final papers both to celebrate the excellent use of language and to read one more time with the eye of an editor.

7

Invitations to Feed Our Writing

Day Four, Choice Unit

Class time filled with independent reading and writing is the heart of the free-choice unit. Everyday students find interesting, well-written passages and flag them with Post-It notes for future reference. Today, the fourth day of the unit, Tracy starts with one of her own, an excerpt from *The Kite Runner* by Khaled Hosseini, sharing it from an overhead transparency at the front of the classroom.

> A month after the wedding, the Taheris, Sharif, his wife Suzy, and several of Soraya's aunts came over to our apartment for dinner. Soraya made *sabzi challow*—white rice with spinach and lamb. After dinner, we all had green tea and played cards in groups of four. Soraya and I played with Sharif and Suzy on the coffee table, next to the couch where Baba lay under a wool blanket. He watched me joking with Sharif, watched Soraya and me lacing our fingers together, watched me push back a loose curl of her hair. I could see his internal smile, as wide as the skies of Kabul on nights when the poplars shivered and the sound of crickets swelled in the gardens.
>
> Just before midnight, Baba asked me to help him into bed. Soraya and I placed his arms on our shoulders and wrapped ours around his back. When we lowered him, he had Soraya turn off the bedside lamp. He asked us to lean in, gave us each a kiss.
>
> "I'll come back with your morphine and a glass of water, Kaka jan," Soraya said.
>
> "Not tonight," he said. "There is no pain tonight."
>
> "Okay," she said. She pulled up the blanket. We closed the door. Baba never woke up. (173)

Tracy reads the passage through twice, the second time encouraging students to examine closely the various ways Hosseini used technique to affect emotion and reader involvement. By this point, the students are accustomed to looking closely at prose. They look at details that are provided: the dinner of rice, spinach, and lamb; the names of guests; the length of time since the wedding; the fact that Kaka jan requires morphine for pain.

Students discuss how much information the author has packed into a short passage: that Soraya and the narrator are newlyweds who take care of Baba (Kaka jan); that Soraya is the cook, and from inference, a good one; that the newlyweds demonstrate their affection in many small, tender gestures—such as lacing fingers together and the husband (narrator) pushing back a lock of her hair.

Finally, they observe the writing itself, noting the ways that Hosseini draws the reader directly into the piece with precise description and use of metaphor, helping her visualize the scene from the inside.

- The protectiveness of Sharif and Suzy for Baba who lies on the couch beside them "under a wool blanket."
- The metaphoric description of Baba's smile.

The author crafts the paragraphs through varying sentence structure. Some sentences start with introductory phrases that give the reader a sense of transition, of time passing.

- A month after the wedding,
- After dinner,
- Just before midnight,

They observe how each of these phrases is set off with a comma from the body of the sentence, giving the phrase emphasis. They note how Hosseini, like Wiesel, varies sentence lengths for dramatic impact. They point to two specific examples in the passage.

> He watched me joking with Sharif, watched Soraya and me lacing our fingers together, watched me push back a loose curl of her hair. I could see his internal smile, as wide as the skies of Kabul on nights when the poplars shivered and the sound of crickets swelled in the gardens.

And, in the final lines of the passage

> She pulled up the blanket. We closed the door. Baba never woke up.

In the first example, the author uses a sentence of twenty-four words followed by a sentence of twenty-eight words. Students observe how these lengthy sentences, filled with details, slow down the reading whereas the final set of four sentences contains a total of sixteen words, the longest having only five words. The longer sentences provide two sophisticated examples of sentence structure that some of the students can now describe: the first with a series of three repetitions of the same strong active verb—watched; the second with the metaphor made up of a long dependent clause. In contrast to the long sentences, the short, simple sentences that end the passage bring the reading to an abrupt, stunning stop.

There are also quick observations about questions the passage raises. Because this is an excerpt, students wonder about the circumstance of Baba living with Soraya and the narrator. Why as newlyweds have they taken on the care of Baba? How did Baba become ill? Is he a relative?

Today, a substantial block of time is set aside for workshop, so students move quickly into the tasks at hand, each using the remainder of the time for their individual writing. Reading rich examples of writing feeds the students' sense of craft and technique. Today as they continue with their independent reading and writing, Tracy announces that she will visit with each of them briefly to check on progress with their writing, discuss any difficulties they may be experiencing, and plan for resources to support them. In-process drafts are due for initial responses from writing groups by early next week, but response conference with peers or teacher can be held at any time.

Plans for Day Four, Choice Unit (day fifteen of the semester)	
Time	**Tasks**
12:05–12:30	Minilesson: observing strong writing features.
12:30–1:25	Reading and writing workshop time.
1:25–1:40	Closing share.

Day Five, Choice Unit

Immediately after students enter the room and settle in with their groups, Tracy shares a favorite picture book with them, *The Giving Tree*, by Shel Silverstein. Before she reads she asks students to pay attention to the way the story is constructed, specifically how the author develops the story from beginning to final resolution. She uses the picture book as an opportunity to review the elements of a story: character, setting, conflict, plot, theme, rising tension or action, resolution, conclusion. As the students talk about these elements in relation to the story, they also focus attention on familiar elements such as point of view, leads, pacing of the action as developed by varying sentence structures.

Tracy directs them to the writing invitation for the day. This pattern has become predictable, so notebooks are close at hand.

Writing Invitation 9

Tell me a story. It can be completely true, completely made up, or somewhere in between. You decide. You can use a genre of your choice to get the words and the story on the page. This means you can tell your story in the form of a poem, short story, essay, news article, drama, script, etc. You'll have ten minutes to write; use all of it. If you do any sketching or outlining, I'll want you to turn that in with the fastwrite. Do your best.

In addition to getting their writing fluency flowing for the day and giving them practice writing under timed conditions in response to a prompt, Tracy will take up these fastwrites for a quick check on growth in writing skills and craft. As before, she uses the student writing to determine areas for continued instruction that will be provided through micro- and minilessons that will be offered either for the whole class, for a small group, or for an individual student. Celly writes,

"Come on! Let's go ride that one!"

"No! That's way too high! I don't want to ride that! Oh look, let's ride that one instead. I love the ones that go around and round. They made me dizzy."

"Hey, that's so childish. Only little girls and boys ride that. Are you a little girl?"

In the midst of hundreds—maybe thousands—of people walking or even running hurriedly to the new row of lines, the two girls started arguing, pausing only long enough to glance up toward a figure high in the sky above. It was colorful, like it was made of metal, and it stood out bigger than anything else. The two girls continued arguing, neither willing to give in to the other, until suddenly they stopped. Both sets of eyes caught sight of . . .

Her fastwrite opens with dialogue, builds using varying sentence structure, introduces an element of concern with the metal figure seen high above, and ends abruptly leaving the reader puzzling about the story coming up. Will it be science fiction? A mystery? A narrative about the exploits of the two girls? Even in this first-draft timed writing, it is clear that the author is trying on a number of strategies learned in class.

Zane takes a different direction. He writes

It was dark, but I didn't need light to see it. I could picture in my mind every table and chair, bookshelf, and bed. From my warm, dark nest I could get up, walk over, and pick out a book, find my clothes, know exactly where to reach to hit the off button on my alarm clock. The moment I put my first arm outside of my nest, I knew it would be much better to remain than to get up.

Zane does many things well. His sentence structure is inviting and varied. The use of specific words and details takes the reader into the scene, and the interesting choice of the word *nest* leaves the reader wondering if this use suggests anything about the character or events to come.

As with the previous class, this one provides a large block of dedicated writing and reading time. As Tracy moves around the room checking in with students on their writing progress, she finds them at various stages of completion. Some have started several pieces, only to lose interest in further developing them at this time. These starts are in the students' writing folders. Others have moved ahead quickly, developing a totally new piece or building from one of the writing invitations or possibilities identified earlier in the semester.

Abby confesses that she hasn't had time to write creatively for a long time, and her mind is reeling with possibilities as a result of having time now: her draft reveals a bizarre story of a woman who is being brainwashed by a subliminal message on a compact disk that accompanies a would-be diet program.

Celly became intrigued with her family's history while researching and writing her earlier nonfiction paper, a portion of the biography of her grandmother who was born in Pyongyang, North Korea, in 1927. Now, she finds herself drawn toward a continuation of that narrative as she continues researching the immigration of her grandparents to the United States.

Barry is a poet. Given the opportunity, he often writes poems and this assignment gives him the invitation to weave poetry and prose, drawing from and building on some of his earlier work, hence his working title: "Up from the Vault." As they visit, Tracy encourages him to read selections from Natalie Ginsburg who uses techniques that Barry might find helpful.

Linda loves artistic representations, so a photograph anchors her emerging work (see Figure 7.1). Her first draft opens with a person sitting at a counter in a diner, sipping coffee. Even in this early draft she draws upon many of the effective strategies she has admired in other pieces of text. Revision is a continuous process for her, too, as is evidenced by the bits of text that are marked through, the vocabulary she identifies for use, the dialogue that is bracketed to come back to later (see Figure 7.2).

In the course of an hour, Tracy moves from one soft conversation to the next as she makes notes on the State of the Class sheet for each student. Students work individually for the most part, anxious to ready their writing for input by the next class, which will be the last one for the week. With minutes to go, Tracy interrupts the work in progress for final questions and a reminder that it would be very helpful to have a draft far enough along for peer response on Friday. Most will want to designate time over the weekend to refine their pieces in anticipation of the scheduled Reading Jam—a community sharing/feedback event for their writing—scheduled as the culmination of the unit next week.

Figure 7.1. Linda's Photo Prompt

Plans for Day Five, Choice Unit (day sixteen of the semester)	
Time	**Tasks**
12:05–12:30	Minilesson: *The Giving Tree* and review of elements of short stories.
12:30–1:25	Reading and writing workshop time.
1:25–1:40	Closing share.

Day Six, Choice Unit

A flurry of activity always comes with the end of the week. With the free-choice pieces due next week for sharing and students wearing an air of seriousness, Tracy chooses a light invitation to get their writing started. They have studied effective use of metaphor and other types of figurative language already. Today, she greets them with examples of exquisitely bad "teen metaphors" drawn from a popular website (http://jumbojoke.com).

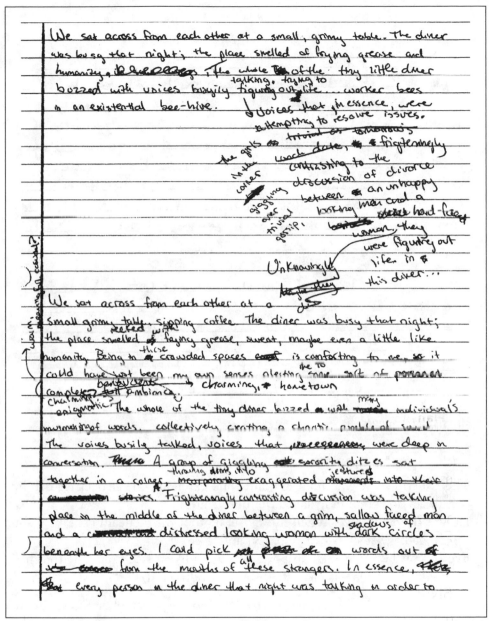

We sat across from each other at a small, grimy table. The diner
was busy that night; the place smelled of frying grease and
humanity. The whole of the tiny little diner
buzzed with voices busily figuring out life... worker bees
in an existential bee-hive. Voices that, in essence, were
attempting to resolve issues.
the girls frighteningly
contrasting to the
discussion of divorce
between an unhappy
looking man and a hard-faced
woman, they
were figuring out
life in
Unknowingly this diner...

We sat across from each other at a
small grimy table, sipping coffee. The diner was busy that night;
the place smelled of frying grease, sweat, maybe even a little like
humanity. Being in these crowded spaces is comforting to me, it
could have just been my own senses alerting me to
charming, hometown
enigmatic. The whole of the tiny diner buzzed with many individual's
murmurs of words, collectively creating a chaotic
The voices busily talked, voices that were deep in
conversation. A group of giggling sorority ditzes sat
together in a corner, incorporating exaggerated gestures into their
stories. Frighteningly contrasting discussion was taking
place in the middle of the diner between a grim, sallow faced man
and a distressed looking woman with dark circles
beneath her eyes. I could pick words out
from the mouths of all these strangers. In essence,
every person in the diner that night was talking in order to

Figure 7.2. Linda's First Draft

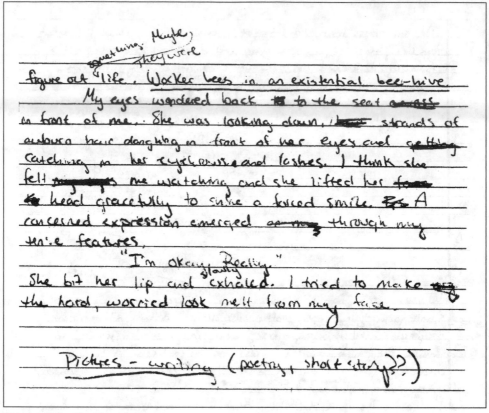

something; Maybe,
they were

figure out "life. Worker bees in an existential bee-hive.
My eyes wandered back to the seat across
in front of me. She was looking down, strands of
auburn hair dangling in front of her eyes and getting
catching in her eyebrows and lashes. I think she
felt me watching and she lifted her
head gracefully to smile a forced smile. A
concealed expression emerged or my through my
tense features.
          "I'm okay, Really."
                    slowly
She bit her lip and exhaled. I tried to make
the hard, worried look melt from my face.

Pictures - writing (poetry, short story??)

Figure 7.2. *Continued*

The ballerina rose gracefully en pointe and extended one slender leg behind
her, like a dog at a fire hydrant. (Jennifer Hart)
He was deeply in love. When she spoke, he thought he heard bells, as if she
were a garbage truck backing up. (Susan Reece)
Even in his last years Grandpappy had a mind like a steel trap, one that had
been left out so long, it had rusted shut. (Sandra Hull)

Using these examples, Tracy reviews the definition of a metaphor and simile in a
microlesson. In pairs, students glance through favorite passages of their books to
find and share effective metaphors and similes, and then offer favorite examples
with the class. Together, they quickly brainstorm some characteristics these similes
and metaphors share.

unexpected comparisons or pairings
ironic

catches you off guard
random or ridiculous pairings
unique perspective
pairing the familiar with the unfamiliar

Tracy sets the stage for a quick writing invitation.

Writing Invitation 10
Brainstorm a list of familiar objects with which you have come in contact to-day. Use these objects, plus others you want, to construct your own examples of outrageous metaphors.

Lists grow rapidly.

- hot dogs, turkey sandwich, oatmeal, Life breakfast cereal, orange juice, sweet and spicy sauce, French fries, rice, a half-full bottle of water, bagel
- sunshine, trees, germs
- car, pencil, shower knobs, door, gray car by the dumpster, balloons
- video on mammals, email, friends

Students take several minutes to write sentences, and even before Tracy brings the group together, they begin to share with partners.

I flew like a dancer moving to the music of a grand piano, the lock of our eyes my spotlight. (Lily)
Knowledge seeped into my head like tar through a sponge. (Christopher)
Her scream sounded like fourteen cats falling down an elevator shaft. (Stan)
The kid ran across the field, a crack addict on speed. (Allison)
The sauce was spicy against my tongue like 500 little knives jabbing into it. (Celly)

The sharing brings smiles from students and encouragement from Tracy to try to include examples of effective metaphors in the pieces under completion. As students settle in for a half hour of uninterrupted work, Tracy reminds them of due dates. A near-final draft is due on Monday for editing groups. On Wednesday and Friday, the final drafts will all go public as students participate in a Reading Jam—an event that provides the opportunity to both share their work with an audience and receive response. On Friday students will turn in a portfolio including final and rough drafts, a Dear Tracy reflective letter discussing their project, and logs for their reading and writing.

Today's thanks and apologies session is filled with comments appreciative of responses received. Students have identified areas of talent in their classroom, and many freely seek advice when they get stuck, find themselves wrestling with a difficult passage, or even need to check a question of mechanics. Tracy sends them into the weekend with a reminder of how eager she is to see their final drafts next week.

Plans for Day Six, Choice Unit (day seventeen of the semester)	
Time	**Tasks**
1:30–1:45	Writing Invitation 10: outrageous metaphors.
1:45–2:15	Workshop time.
2:15–2:30	Thanks and apologies.

Taking a Step Back

This semester's work continues to demonstrate a shift in responsibility from the teacher to the students for reading and writing growth as students are encouraged continuously to make more decisions about their own work and to assume a collaborative role with peers. Now, six weeks into the semester, behaviors make it clear that students understand the expectation of respect for the group and collaborative learning has deepened their sense of responsibility to include fellow writers and readers in class who may not be a part of their lives elsewhere.

Every day provides moments to focus closely on elements of written language. Close reading, multiple levels of discussion, and careful analysis of texts bridge the literature being read and writing being composed. Through individual, small group, and whole class discussions and playfully engaging a variety of structures, styles, and devices, students gain the ability to see these for themselves in the materials they choose to read and to use them independently in the various types of writing they pursue. This focus on author's style and language encourages close reading as students become more interested in the ways that authors speak to them.

These moments of focus on particular aspects of writing provide multiple levels for reinforcement. Issues related to use of rules, conventions, style, and craft are discussed and then immediately reinforced as Tracy encourages students to embed particular features in their own work. In addition, notes are stored in the writer's notebook for later reference, either when the issue is up for focus again or as a part of the ongoing writing/revising/editing process.

Tracy continues to study her students' writing to gather cues for future instructional emphasis. This week students have completed a story writing invitation similar to the one completed the first week of class. Placing these side-by-side, Tracy analyzes the pieces to identify episodes of growth. She highlights papers to document use of strategies she has taught and pays attention to the specific needs of individual students.

Approaching teaching this way requires an enormously high level of organization. By maintaining a State of the Class sheet for each student, she can see at a glance details about progress in reading and writing. By glancing at the students' writing notebooks, she can tell much about the ongoing processing of writing ideas and techniques. And by looking over the students' reading and writing logs, she has a detailed overview that illustrates their writing and reading behaviors in and out of school.

Such ongoing assessment provides a wealth of information to support data-driven decision making at every step along the way. Further, by providing students opportunities to seamlessly move from writing laced with choice—in topic, genre, pace, and length—to "writing on demand"—focused, timed writing in response to prompts—Tracy prepares them to address the requirements of various tests that loom before them (Gere, Christenbury, and Sassi 2005).

As essential as organization is, it would be of little value without the professional expertise of the teacher. The notion of adopting someone else's curriculum or pacing guide would be a waste in a workshop classroom in which the teacher must not only know the "basics" involved in writing instruction but must also be able to anticipate the needs of the writer. Because this teacher is a writer herself, she is in a position to understand, anticipate, and navigate her students' needs. In fact, by keeping a close eye on the students' reading and writing, she is able to place new areas of language emphasis before them along the way, just in time for their next draft.

8

Emerging Drafts

Day Seven, Choice Unit

A hum of activity begins even before the bell has rung to signal the start of class. Students know that today is the day to push for completion of papers, a day set aside for multitiered response to their writing although most students have already sought out and drawn on response over the past two weeks. With seriousness, they prepare their text today for the public sharing at the class Reading Jam, scheduled for the next two class periods, Wednesday and Friday.

"Start with a conference with yourself," Tracy reminds them. "And don't take yourself too lightly! You can provide some of the best response to your work yourself!" Though a familiar feature by now, she reminds students of the procedures for self-conferencing.

- Find a spot where you feel comfortable reading aloud.
- Settle in and read your own paper slowly, emphasizing each word.
- Listen for sentences that don't flow as well as they should, gaps in the narrative that you realize might raise questions for a reader, words that sound flat, that don't seem to move the piece along or fail to offer crisp, precise description that will help a reader see and feel from the inside. Don't stop to make changes, but note or circle anything you think you might want to come back to.
- Pull out the skills sheet that you've been keeping in your notebook. Remember, these are the skills that you and I have agreed that you need to work on for this paper. Read your paper through a second time checking it carefully for these skills.
- Finally, go back into the paper. Let your editing notes direct your revisions. Make changes by adding new material directly to the draft, drawing arrows

to move things around, crossing out things that need to go away. Be sure all the changes are clear to you so they provide a guide for your final draft.

Some students aren't ready for the conference with themselves. Instead, they need more time for drafting, or they need to seek advice from another writer or Tracy. Others, who have already worked through several drafts, are eager to move into final revision.

Linda has six handwritten drafts already, each a patchwork of reworking to get exactly the desired effect. As seen earlier, she started with a simple scene of a couple sitting across from one another at a table in a diner, a scene triggered from a photo. Linda likes philosophy, and as early as the second draft, she begins to weave in a new dimension to the scene, a reflection on Aristotle and his notions of actuality and fulfillment. By her third draft, the veil of philosophy has settled on the characters in the diner. Not until her sixth draft does she shift the dialogue in the first scene to her lead; she'll maintain and tighten this in her final draft.

In each new draft she works the language and approach to the first paragraph as she tweaks the opening to tighten the introduction to her characters and scene and help the reader sense the deeper emotions and thoughts behind the simplicity of the diner setting. She moves through her entire paper in this manner, draft after draft.

Today she works from a typed copy of what might be her final draft. In the corner by the window, she sits hovering over the pages, softly reading to herself as she radically attacks this seventh draft (see Figure 8.1). She draws lines to indicate sentences to be inserted. A few lines are marked through, signaling their impending disappearance from the paper. Yet, far more prevalent are the additions to the text. An important part of revision is seeing what isn't there and should be. Careful reading of the paper aloud to herself helps Linda think about the words as a reader might receive them.

Several areas for work are noted on Linda's skills and craft sheet. Among them she comes across a goal to attend to interesting sentence structure: to try using shortened sentences sometimes for dramatic effect; to use semicolons to link ideas in sentences; to experiment with dialogue to pull the reader into a narrative faster. In her second reading of the draft, she glances at the skills and craft sheet, then back at her paper, and makes more notes for changes.

Linda spends almost an hour working alone before she joins a response group. Members of the group listen carefully to each other, and after each reading they briefly discuss effective parts of the paper, areas where they are unsure of something, places where wording raises a question. After each person has had the opportunity to read aloud and receive verbal feedback, the students pass the papers round the group of four. Each student reads and comments on the papers from

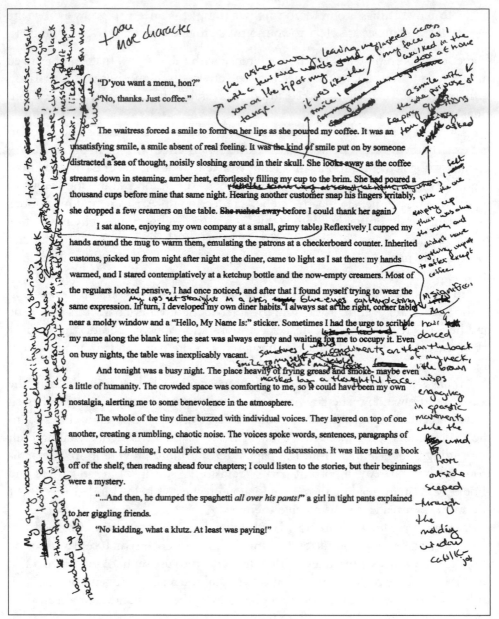

Figure 8.1. Linda's Seventh Draft

118

the other three students. This final response includes suggestions for editing. If the writer is comfortable with notes being made directly on the draft, partners do so. Otherwise, notes go on stickies that are available for that purpose.

Stan has worked with three story ideas during the choice unit, starting with a draft he describes as "almost sandpapery in texture," that overviews each of his three ideas. All emerge from stories his dad has shared. He has settled on a Vietnam story that he entitled "Flag Pole Stroll," an account of his dad caught in a mortar attack in the dead of night. Despite the gravity of the scene and events, Stan finds it possible to inject humor as his dad races through camp in the darkness and collides with the only flag pole in the area.

Today, several drafts into the piece, Stan settles into conference with himself on a draft that has grown from a single paragraph to over three typed pages. In particular, he is interested today in checking that his paragraphing "doesn't ramble on with unnecessary description or content," a goal taken from his skills and craft sheet. He appreciates crisp writing, and he's trying to develop sharp descriptions of characters and events. After reading and revising on his own, he, too, is ready for a response group and a quick conference with Tracy.

Both Stan and his response partners make notes directly on his paper, as illustrated by his first page of text (see Figure 8.2): suggestions for a change of verb; ideas on paragraphing adjustments; notations on places where the text could be tightened or expanded. The group works quickly, allowing time for Stan to have a three-minute conference with Tracy who writes

> Stan—I love this story. I think that your energy at the end ran short. There was so much more to write. Your editing comments are superb. Bravo! Your dialogue format is incorrect. Please read the notes from your skills sections and see me if you have any questions. Your writing has a strong voice and excellent descriptions. I'm really proud of the editing comments you've made. Keep them in mind as you redo this for your final draft. Critically looking at your own work will help your writing grow at an alarming rate! You can do it!

Tracy laces constructive comments with celebration; because the comments are specific, Stan is armed with precise ways to strengthen his prose.

By this point many of the members of the class are able to work with minimal teacher guidance, freeing Tracy to work more closely with the students who struggle with their writing. Early in the class period, she moves from one student to the next, offering individual instruction and support. Later, she assembles a group of four in one corner of the room, sitting with them and modeling as they practice responding to one another's work. As time permits, she joins other response groups, as she did with Stan's, to participate in the written response process.

By the end of the class period, Linda, Stan, and all the other students are well into final revision and editing of their own papers, using suggestions from peer

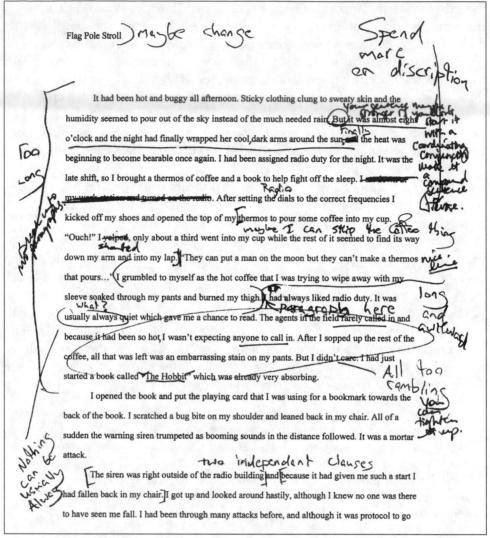

Figure 8.2. Stan's Near Final Version

groups as they deem important; final decisions about what to adjust and owner-ship for the writing remains with the writer. Final revisions will be completed outside of class. Tracy spends the final minutes of the period describing the Reading Jam coming up on Wednesday and Friday. Each student will be given the opportunity to be the "invited artist" as they read their original work, or a por-tion of a longer piece, to the class. Each member of the audience will provide written notes in response to each piece read, so the authors can anticipate having written feedback from each of their peers and from the adults in the room.

Because of the number of students and length of some pieces, Tracy has set aside two days for the Reading Jam. The final day, the short class for the week, will be the due date for papers, which will be turned in with all drafts to illustrate revisions, self-evaluation letters, and skills and craft sheets.

Plans for Day Seven, Choice Unit (day eighteen of the semester)	
Time	**Tasks**
12:05–1:30	Revision and editing workshop time (students use time initially for conference with self, then for revision/response groups). Tracy works with individual and small groups.
1:30–1:40	Preparation for Reading Jam.

Days Eight and Nine, Choice Unit

The Reading Jam fills the last two days of this free-choice unit, offering authors the opportunity to share final pieces with an audience of interested listeners. As the students enter for the first day of the Jam, they find the center front of the classroom set up like a café where a poetry reading might take place. Students settle in as Tracy shares important information about the final self-evaluation and writing attitude survey for the project. She explains,

> Self-evaluation is essential to me as a writer because it helps me to reflect on my writing, to come to a deeper understanding of it, and to set future goals. I want you to go inside of your own writing so you too can better understand yourself as a writer.
>
> I want you to write me a letter about your observations about this piece of writing and its development. You should use a standard letter format with "Dear Tracy" as your header. You will want to use paragraphs, vary your sentence structure, and let your voice come through.

Together, the class brainstorms the types of information that would be most helpful in a self-evaluation letter, and Tracy captures thoughts from around the room on an overhead transparency.

> strengths and weaknesses as I see them
> how well I captured the true feelings I intended
> lines that I really like
> lines I'm not happy with yet

thoughts about how effective the capitalization, punctuation, and usage are
whether there's any dialogue; whether dialogue is used effectively
my own feeling about the piece
who I'm planning to share this with
what I learned—even if I don't feel the piece is great
thoughts about my process—what worked and what should be changed

The completed self-evaluation letter and a follow-up writing attitude survey will be included in the final portfolio of papers due at the next class.

One more thing is important before the Jam commences. Each student has collected a stack of pastel shaded blank notes. These will be used to provide written feedback to each student as they share. Tracy reminds students about the type of response they have agreed previously to be helpful: comments that are honest, respectful, and specific. She encourages students to offer comments that focus on positive features of the work and, if they identify an area they think may improve with more revision, to note a wish for the piece.

One by one, students volunteer to take the chair up front, beginning by telling a little bit about themselves and then about the writing.

- Elizabeth shares a poem about her grandmother who was an Auschwitz survivor
- Barry, a poem about cream soda, heavy with sexual images
- Celly, a narrative about a magic ring that houses a fairy named Ella, a gift from her Granny just before the elder woman's death
- Thomas, a true story rich with dialogue and detail
- Abby, a highly textured character development
- Allison, a photo collage with poems

Linda's short philosophical excerpt provides an excellent example of how active revision can result in a tighter, more compact piece of writing. Now into her eighth draft, the description of her diner scene has deepened and her conclusion has shifted to reflect the philosophic stance she has worked so hard to achieve (see Figure 8.3). Further, her piece has evolved from a rambling multipage paper to two and one-half pages of tightly written prose.

As her concluding paragraph lingers in the air, it is met quickly with spontaneous applause. Written notes for Linda capture many of the facets of the writing that peers appreciated.

I love your photography! That was awesome. I got so much imagery from it. Beautifully worded. I love the link to the beehive as well!
The piece was so interesting. Do you read a lot of philosophy? Worker bees in an existential beehive . . . sounds cool.

"D'you want a menu, hon?"

"No, thanks. Just coffee."

The waitress forced a smile to form on her lips as she poured my coffee. It was an unsatisfying smile, a smile absent of real feeling. It was the kind of smile put on by someone distracted by a sea of thought, noisily sloshing around in their skull. It was the smile I plastered across my face so my parents wouldn't ask me how my day went. The smile that had the sole purpose of deceptive happiness. She looks away as the coffee streams down in steaming, amber heat, effortlessly filling my cup to the brim. She had poured a thousand cups before mine that same night. Hearing another customer snap his fingers irritably, she dropped a few creamers on the table. Before I could thank her again, she rushed away, leaving me with my kind words gone sour at the tip of my tongue. Regret leaked into my open mouth, and I wished I could have thanked her again, because it might have transformed the forced smile to a genuine one.

I sat alone, enjoying my own company at a small, grimy table. I tried to imagine how I looked to the other people at the diner; cryptic exhaustion marked by dark circles under my black eyelashes, concealed by a mess of brown bangs, in need of a trim, that fell into my eyes. I liked to think my eyes were an electrifying, mysterious shade of blue; a cerulean blue that could see right through a person without recognizing the matter of the person in front of them. The grey hoodie I wore tonight was threadbare, fading poetically around the shoulders and pockets so that peeks of red showed through from my rolling stones tee-shirt. The grey, familiar fabric was bunched up around my neck, tickled by my short hair, while the sleeves cocooned my hands, cold from the icy temperature outside. Reflexively I cupped my hands around the mug to warm them, emulating the patrons at a checkerboard counter.

Inherited customs, picked up from night after night at the diner, came to light as I sat there: my hands warmed, and I stared contemplatively at a ketchup bottle and the now-empty creamers. The door opened with a burst of frigidly cold air; the wind engaged my bangs in a spastic tango, then squeezed underneath my clothing to give me goose bumps. Whoever had just come in was already lost amongst the seated figures inside; he was probably another habitual diner customer. My goose bumps receded back into my skin and I focused my eyes again, not noticing that I had been scanning the crowd. Most of the regulars looked pensive, I had once noticed, and after

Figure 8.3. Linda's Eight Draft

that I found myself trying to wear the same expression. My lips were set straight, blue eyes contemplating insignificant condiments on the table, or re-reading the posters and stickers I had become so familiar with. Sometime I smile to myself, realizing how much older I must appear to the patrons, masked by a thoughtful face when, truthfully, I was living for the here and now, in the diner. In turn, I developed my own diner habits. I always sat at the right, corner table, near a moldy window and a "Hello, My Name Is:" sticker. Sometimes I had the urge to scribble my name along the blank line; the seat was always empty and waiting for me to occupy it. Even on busy nights, the table was inexplicably vacant.

And tonight was a busy night. The place smelled heavily of frying grease and smoke—maybe even a little of humanity. The crowded space was comforting to me, so it could have been my own nostalgia, alerting me to some benevolence in the atmosphere.

The whole of the tiny diner buzzed with individual voices. They layered on top of one another, creating a rumbling, chaotic noise. The voices spoke words, sentences, paragraphs of conversation. Listening, I could pick out certain voices and discussions. It was like taking a book off of the shelf, then reading ahead four chapters; I could listen to the stories, but their beginnings were a mystery.

". . . And then, he dumped the spaghetti *all over his pants!*" a girl in tight pants explained to her giggling friends.

"No kidding, what a klutz. At least he was paying!"

"Seriously, I am **so** glad I never called him back," the girl stated haughtily. I winced at her superficiality. She sounded like my mother, on a tangent concerning the date she had just returned home from. The only differences were my mother's relatively more extensive vocabulary and that the receiving end of the tangent, me, wasn't really ever listening. Or caring.

At the counter, sleazy men lost in blankets of cigarette smoke chatted loudly. A young couple passed a pair of ratty headphones between them over a plate of onion rings. They smiled at each other when the volume jumped up during a track, and laughed when their eyes met, making me wish I knew the songs, knew the feeling of catching someone's gaze and clasping it for as long as I could. Behind them, old men talked about the past while fresh-faced college kids speculated about the future.

I read once about a branch of Aristotle's philosophy, called *Nicomachean Ethics*. He claims that all human beings want happiness, so that "one can

Figure 8.3. *Continued*

realize a sense of actuality and fulfillment." I felt a little like a disciple of his, sitting in the corner, psychoanalyzing other's conversations. My contemplative mask was tightly fastened, my hands cradled the coffee cup, my tousled brown hair and vivid blue eyes, blending smoothly with the diner's inhabitants. I had my metaphorical frequent visitor's pass, wadded up inside the folds of my grey hoodie, within my expression, deep under the grime on the table and the dirty fibers of the chair. And now, with some Aristotelean ESP, I could interpret the discussions. All of them broke down into simple concepts. Resolving ambivalence. Choosing paths. Receiving feedback. Obtaining happiness. Figuring out *life*. They were worker bees in an existential beehive.

Figure 8.3. *Continued*

I really appreciate the first lines where it's a dialogue and thought process. The piece is short, yet meaningful.
Wow, very impressive! You sound very smart. It's cool how you take someone like Aristotle and his philosophy and make it a story.

After Linda's reading, members of the audience write quick responses and then share aloud for a few moments. Notes then thread their way to her from across the class containing consistent references to her use of photography as a link to her writing, to her effective introduction that uses dialogue to drop the reader into the piece, and to her conclusion that frames the prose with philosophic reflection and a powerful metaphor.

Each reader receives this immediate and specific feedback and reinforcement. Moreover, the types of comments provide evidence of the effectiveness of the various micro- and minilessons as well. Students are incorporating many of the techniques and devices that have been taught into their writing. In addition, it is clear through the written feedback that they are able to recognize and appreciate the use of these techniques in the writing of peers.

By the end of the final day of the unit, all students have had a moment in the spotlight. Like a stack of valentines, each reader has received notes from members of their audience and enjoyed reading about the things peers consider effective in the choice piece of writing. Certainly the variety of topics and genres attests to the unique needs and interests of students as they approach such an assignment.

Still, even the freedom and support given do not prevent some feelings of trepidation. Her Dear Tracy letter finds Linda tracking her path through her paper's development and wondering if she went off course along the way. She second guesses the effectiveness of her photographs, wonders about when and why she moved from developing poems to developing a narrative, muses about the connection—or lack of connection—she senses between some of her photographs and her final paper.

Linda does feel confident in the effectiveness of some of her lines; in particular, the final beehive metaphor is one she loves. Overall, though, she notes that "I *know* I could have done better, so I'll probably end up going back to it later and achieving what I wanted with it." These are the words of a writer. Even the final draft isn't finished, and there's always room to strengthen the writing more.

Plans for Day Eight, Choice Unit (day nineteen of the semester)	
Time	**Tasks**
12:05–12:25	Review of self-evaluation expectations. Brainstorm of helpful self-evaluation information.
12:25–12:40	Preparation for Reading Jam.
12:40–1:40	Reading Jam, sharing of written responses.

Plans for Day Nine, Choice Unit (day twenty of the semester)	
Time	**Tasks**
12:05–12:15	Review of portfolio pieces to be submitted at end of period.
12:15–12:35	Reading Jam, sharing of written responses.
12:35–12:40	Final check of portfolio pieces. Turn in portfolio.

Taking a Step Back

The final week of the first free-choice unit for the semester mirrors the processes and procedures Tracy established during the first days of class. Because of the predictability of opportunities for writing in class, for gathering and giving feedback, and for using the response of peers and adults in the room, students count on these instructional opportunities and use them to advantage. Without this predictability and routine, they wouldn't know what to anticipate, a circumstance that could quickly remove power and responsibility for planning ahead. In short, for students to be creative and to make maximum use of the class time provided for real work, they need a predictable environment with predictable routines.

This last week has provided ample evidence of the varying writing processes and interests of students. For some, writing is a matter of reading, and reading, and reading . . . and finally sitting down to write in a mighty rush. These writers seem to pour a complete first draft on to the page and, like sculptors, revise by freeing the final paper from the rough stone within which it resides. For others, writing is more a process of crafting draft after draft, slowly, carefully tinkering with language and technique. The workshop allows this variation and encourages students to recognize and build on the processes that work most productively for them.

There is no magic formula in the workshop that prescribes how many drafts or how long the final draft must be. There is, however, a strong emphasis on self-awareness and self-reflection. Self-awareness frequently translates to a sense of self as a writer in a community of writers, an understanding that writing is both a personal and an intensely social act. By the time students get to the high school classroom, some have had years of bad experiences with writing and, unfortunately, associate it with pain—not pleasure—resulting in reluctance to share their work. As a result of the dozens of little steps structured to build community and provide interested, authentic audiences among peers, most find themselves willing—even eager—to have their words listened to by others.

Throughout the choice unit, students experienced latitude in deciding when to seek collaboration, when to work alone, and when they needed to go back into their reading for inspiration. They didn't start at the same level of proficiency and comfort with writing; they didn't move at the same pace; nor did they all produce publishable pieces. But they did all produce multiple drafts of pieces they were proud to share and able to critique. This in itself reflects remarkable progress.

As important as the individual pieces of writing are, ultimately they are artifacts—and better ones than students could have developed without opportunities to work through drafts with the support of collaborators. Nonetheless, as noted by Katie Wood Ray (2004) when describing the work of very young writers, the importance must be placed on improving the writer, not just an individual piece of writing.

How do we know that the writer is better? More successful? We'll describe more about this in the next section when we examine the question, "But does it really work?" There we'll unpack the portfolio of papers to look for evidence of growth. We'll examine the students' use of skills and craft techniques from the lessons they have experienced. We'll look more closely at their attitudes, interests, and investment in their work.

On the last day of the Reading Jam, students assemble portfolios of their papers. The bundles move from their hands to Tracy's and from hers to the basket that will define her weekend ahead. As the students move from the classroom and off to weekend activities of their own, Tracy catches my eye and remarks, "Even with the best of intentions, there's still the grade at the end of the process."

Tracy's comment underscores the awkward dance that is the metaphor of the workshop. Despite the modeling of the best practices we know that are fashioned to offer our students choice, ownership, process, time, and authentic feedback, there is still the defining quality of school with which we struggle. The workshop offers us the chance to invite the students into the life of the writer. Once they have experienced the power of their own words, we hope they'll never look back.

Part 4

· · · · · ·

But Does This Really Work?

In the first three parts of this book, we've taken down the walls of a single classroom to allow a peek inside as a high school teacher moves students into a new delivery model for writing and reading, one requiring more personal and collaborative responsibility than most of the students had experienced previously. In Part 1, we looked closely at how that sense of responsibility was developed as students engaged in multiple acts of community building. In Parts 2 and 3, we examined the ways in which core values of a workshop classroom were woven into the fabric of the instruction—values such as real time for reading and writing in and outside of the classroom, multiple opportunities to give and receive feedback, strategic lessons specifically designed to meet needs and extend knowledge of writing craft and skills, and ongoing opportunities for choice of topic or genre.

The representative units offer a template for semester-long planning while genre study and choice units continue to spiral through the semester with each directed genre study taking students into a different subgenre of nonfiction.

Unit One/Week One: Building community and routines
Unit Two/Weeks Two–Four: Directed genre study
Unit Three/Weeks Five–Seven: Choice
Unit Four/Weeks Eight–Ten: Directed genre study
Unit Five/Weeks Eleven–Thirteen: Choice
Unit Six/Weeks Fourteen–Fifteen: Directed genre study (personal essays for tests and college applications)
Unit Seven/Weeks Sixteen–Eighteen: Choice

Allowing so much student interaction, movement, choice, and individualization might give rise to questions about the benefits of this type of instructional change. While it cannot be denied that infusing workshop values into the nonfiction classroom led to interesting work for Tracy's students, important questions remain to determine whether the change was worth the effort. As students prepare for exit tests, college entry tests, and the realities of the workplace, we find ourselves left with questions about how well the workshop model prepares them for these challenges. In this section we'll attempt to unpack the following questions.

- What about external expectations? Does a class such as the one described adequately prepare the students for the articulated expectations of local curriculum and state and national standards? Will the students be prepared for the requirements of high stakes state testing? For college predictor tests such as the SAT and the ACT?

- Does it work for students? Do they really grow as writers? Do they find writing more engaging? Do they show more willingness to put in the hard work it takes to become more proficient as writers?

- And, finally, what about the teacher? Clearly, setting up and facilitating a class such as this one is a huge amount of work. How has this worked for Tracy, a mom of two young children, who is equally as busy outside of school as she is in?

As we look at each of these questions, we'll do so with the students at the heart of the conversation. Two overarching goals led to Tracy's decision to move workshop values into her pedagogy: to improve the writing of students and to improve the student writers. As we unpack our questions about effectiveness, we'll do so with a sharp look at how the change affects the growth of both the writing and the writer.

9

What About the Curriculum, Standards, and Tests?

Since the advent of the national standards movement almost two decades ago, every state and numerous independent agencies have jumped into the fray, carefully defining the knowledge, skill, and strategy-based competencies that students need to master before leaving high school. These competencies, described as essential for college and workplace success, influence the individual high school teacher and her students in a number of ways. To think about whether a particular instructional model works, it becomes important to think about how well it prepares students for the multitude of demands defined by external agents and funneled into the local classroom.

Though state standards vary in terms of their specific approaches to and impact on instructional expectations, numerous points of similarity exist. Looking at two states that have approached standards implementation in different ways may help to frame our discussion of effectiveness of the nonfiction workshop approach. Some states, such as Michigan, have traditionally framed standards as a resource for public and private schools to help them assess and design curriculum at the local level. Others, such as North Carolina, have used the state standards to articulate a mandated state curriculum that, in turn, drives decisions in local classrooms throughout the state; extensive financial support for staff development and materials has accompanied these decisions. In both cases, standards were developed through a broad-based effort involving teachers, curriculum planners, and university professors who sought to describe knowledge, skills, and competencies needed for success beyond the K–12 program. And, in both cases, various types of performance tests backed up the expectations of the state standards.

When looking at testing, the two states might be looked at as representing opposite ends of a spectrum. In North Carolina, end-of-grade tests are tied to the state mandated curriculum. Because passing these tests is required, high school students feel the full impact of them as high-stakes measures. In Michigan, on the other hand, tests have traditionally taken place at strategic junctures in the K–12 program, and the high school graduation test has only recently been required for all students; further, scholarship support in terms of real dollars has been attached for students who pass all parts of the Michigan High School Proficiency Test. Most recently, this exit test was set aside by the state legislature in favor of the ACT, to be given to all exiting high school students in lieu of any other local test beginning in 2007. When implemented, the standard battery of existing subtests, the writing test, and additional subject-specific tests developed for Michigan will be used.

Despite their differences, both states—in fact most states—have drawn from the same research and theory base in establishing expectations. Both states

- assign specific values for listening, speaking, reading, writing, and critical viewing/media literacy.
- speak of the natural connections among the various language and literacy processes.
- emphasize the importance of writing for a variety of purposes and audiences and in a host of genres, accompanied by instructional support as students move toward greater independence.
- emphasize the critical place of reading for information and for pleasure, stressing the interconnectedness of various genres of text as students read for personal, work-related, and academic purposes.
- stress the importance of gaining proficiency in Standard American English and in using appropriate grammatical and mechanical conventions as appropriate to a selected genre.
- emphasize the critical importance of technology for literacy development in the twenty-first century.
- demonstrate high investment in the belief that competency in literacy is essential for all students.

Individual states are not alone in shaping the conversation about what all students must know and be able to do. Professional organizations such as the National Council of Teachers of English and the International Reading Association led the way with standards that address literacy skills and processes; these standards also stress critical issues of access to materials and technology for all students (see NCTE/IRA standards in Appendix A). Educators working with NCTE have shaped numerous policy statements, including the Beliefs about the Teaching of Writing (see Appendix A) that synthesize many research studies into clear statements that can be used to shape writing instruction. In addition to NCTE and IRA, professional groups such as the National Writing Project (NWP) and others have published rich studies that describe successful practice in the teaching of writing. These studies explain the importance of process approaches; of teaching skills in the context of authentic writing; of writing in a variety of genres, for varied purposes and audiences; and of instruction in strategies that support writers as they move into new rhetorical contexts.

Recently, other external agencies have asserted their voices into the conversation. In 2003 the National Writing Commission issued *The Neglected R*, a report that speaks forcefully for an increased emphasis on writing in the nation's schools. Arguing that "writing is not a frill for the few, but an essential skill for the many" (14), the commission cited growing concern voiced by "education, business, and policy-making communities that the level of writing in the United States is not what it should be" (10). The commission recommends that students spend more time writing than they currently do in school, that more in- and out-of-school assignments focus on writing, and that writing across the curriculum and writing to learn be fully integrated into writing programs (29).

Also, *Ready or Not: Creating a High School Diploma That Counts*, outlines eight very specific benchmarks for English Language Arts deemed essential for college or workplace success. Published in 2004 by Achieve, a nonprofit independent agency created by the National Governor's Conference and national business leaders, and now an influential voice in reviewing and making recommendations for changes to individual state standards, *Ready or Not* provides sixty-two expectations ranging from demonstrating "control of standard English through the use of grammar, punctuation, capitalization and spelling" (31) to writing "an academic essay" (33), to identifying and explaining "the themes found in a single literary work" (37). Espousing a more traditional view of essential literacy skills, the benchmarks nonetheless include recognition of the importance of writing for varying purposes and audiences and in varying genres drawing on a process approach. Further, the ability to revise and edit based on feedback from peers and others is recognized as essential for successful writing.

Finally, though the list could go on for pages more, the College Board, designer of the Scholastic Aptitude Test (SAT), and Academic College Testing, Inc., designers of the ACT, hold growing influence over the teaching of writing in high schools. As major brokers of tests designed to predict future college success, both organizations have taken an active role in clamoring for more and better writing instruction in schools. Major documents, including standards, published by these organizations describe support for heightening student awareness of writing as a process, for developing student ability to make decisions about stylistic and rhetorical aspects of writing, for helping students gain competency in research, and for the appropriate use of grammatical and mechanical conventions in written work.

Clearly, voices many miles from the local high school classroom have a substantial impact on the requirements facing teachers and their students. References to creating curricula that reflects rigor and relevance are common in the published conversation. Thankfully, though various governmental and private agencies have become highly invested in describing what students should know and be able to do, few have involved themselves in prescribing how we accomplish this work.

Tracy, as a representative of good teachers everywhere, started her curricular planning by thinking hard about the needs of her students with all of the external demands and expectations serving as a backdrop to her thinking. She refined her understanding of her students' needs early in the semester as she assessed their demonstrated writing and reading skills through various attitudinal surveys, fastwrites, and responses. Though these informal measures took little instructional time and were integrally woven into the fabric of classroom instruction, they allowed her to identify critical skills that all students would benefit from reviewing. They helped her pinpoint specific needs for skills and craft lessons to meet identified areas of weakness. They helped her to gauge the level of interest in various genres for reading and writing and to determine the abilities of various students to read and comprehend new materials, to make connections, and to transfer knowledge into writing.

Because she is a highly professional teacher, she was keenly aware of the requirements of her local curriculum, her state standards, and the types of skills her students would need to possess to successfully navigate the demands of their high school exit test and the ACT or SAT. Those external expectations provide an umbrella of expectations for her students. She understood, moreover, that rigor and relevance can only be realized if there is also relationship. Bringing these new three R's into the classroom allowed her to fashion a program of study that engaged her students and challenged them to push themselves to meet or exceed expectations and to connect their classroom work with the realities of their lives as members of families and communities beyond the school.

Throughout choice and teacher-articulated units, the emphasis for the semester focused on the development of process, strategies, and contextualized learning. By helping students know how to approach new tasks, draw on varied strategies to generate and organize ideas, move from ideas to paper, and draw on personal and collaborative resources to look at their writing with new perspectives, students have learned to approach new writing situations with greater confidence and with internalized resources. The big payoff: When approaching new genres in English class, in another content area, for a test, or for a college essay, students are better prepared to tackle the demands that confront them.

Throughout the semester, specific value has been placed on authentic use of listening, speaking, reading, and writing. For example, students have practiced listening and speaking in a host of contexts for real purposes. Often, this work has directly related to understanding a text or revising personal work. All four language processes have been integral to capturing important information from mini- and microlessons, storing resources in the writer's notebook, and creating and drawing on resources for use in the future. Over the course of the semester, stress has been placed on reading and writing as social acts: Though we begin by making meaning ourselves, we never make meaning in a vacuum. The thoughts, reactions, and perspectives of others help us to see and think in new ways. Similarly, the reactions and questions of others help us to think of our own writing anew, potentially bringing depth and precision that may not have been possible working alone. Understanding and drawing on the social nature of language, the teacher helps prepare students for using all language processes in workplace and college settings.

The integration of literacy processes has been seamless in the nonfiction workshop. Students learned early that they needed to depend on one another to improve their reading and writing. Reading shared texts, taking time to explore context of events, author circumstances, and social issues, help to bring home the notion that writers compose with intentionality—to share a specific message with an envisioned audience; that writers compose to put particular messages into the world. Stopping often to engage in collaborative close reading of excerpted passages allows opportunities to think about how authors manipulate language to craft a particular message, feeling, or desire. It demonstrates real reasons to think seriously about otherwise tedious aspects of language use such as punctuation and capitalization. Students come to realize that even these features represent choices an author makes deliberately. The continuous movement from examination of writing by experts to experimenting with similar patterns or features in their own writing provides immediate opportunities to make otherwise abstract information personally relevant. Students quickly come to understand that they, too, can create effects with their writing; they, too, could have a voice that might change an opinion or share an insight. This knowledge elevates the role of classroom writing from mundane tasks to opportunities to think about their own messages and the impact of these messages on others.

Virtually every class period has included fastwrites of various sorts. During the very first class of the semester, students completed multiple pieces of writing within the first forty-five minutes. The types of writing changed from day to day and unit to unit, but the challenging pace remained constant. As *The Neglected R* recommends, writing was integral to the work of the classroom everyday. Throughout, the instructional goal was to equip students with resources and tools so that they could approach new situations with a greater sense of power.

Students have learned that reading skills cross genre boundaries. Reading for the purpose of living through the literature helps us touch realities that we could not have touched otherwise. Such experiences also make it possible to dip into one's own experiences, to connect with the lives, circumstances, and dilemmas of others. When the experience is beyond our own, we can live through it with empathy. Reading for pleasure allows us to connect with and gain new knowledge and perspectives and to bring these to bear on our own life and circumstances. Gaining these skills is important for personal success and vital for living in a republic such as ours.

By emphasizing personal choices in reading and encouraging organized sharing of favorite titles and authors, Tracy has built personal reading into the curriculum in an integral way. Certainly students are more aware of the plethora of possible authors, titles, and genres than they would have been had they only read whole class assigned texts. However, the long-term impact is far more than this: Hearing from others they trust—classmates, friends, and adults in their lives—about the books and authors they love provides a driving force that encourages wide reading of texts. For many, this cross-pollination leads to experimentation with genres and exploration of authors previously untouched or unfamiliar. To develop good readers, we must first get readers reading (Early 1960; Allen 1995; Beers 2003). Now that Tracy's students have developed investment, it becomes easy enough to shape and refine the tools they bring to the task. Moreover, the more her students read and talk about texts, the more they have to bring to their own writing.

What do readers read for pleasure? In Tracy's class the choices range from fantasy to sports magazines; from contemporary novels to classics; from newspapers to books of poetry. Significantly, there's a place for fiction and nonfiction as choices for pleasure and informational reading and as parts of whole class instruction. In fact, many texts, while being read for pleasure, are also approached as information sources to help understand a different circumstance or issue. Students learn that most texts can provide both types of reading experiences. Moreover, these texts provide the lenses through which personal writing is envisioned as students experiment with new or less familiar genres. They learn explicitly that, though form and choice of tone and language vary from genre to genre, academic writing does not require sifting out voice and passion to match a preprescribed form. As a result, academic writing—such as essays of various sorts—becomes stronger and more vibrant.

It is one thing to describe how language shifts and changes from one context to another, to explain that different decisions about language are made by writers because those choices carry the intended message more forcefully than any other; it is quite a different and more powerful thing to show how authors make these choices as they craft messages. By moving from Elie Wiesel's memoir to Martin Luther King's speech to poetry by Ralph Fletcher and Sara Holbrook, students see the ways in which choices about language impact message. Of course proficiency in Standard American English and use of appropriate grammatical and mechanical conventions are emphases for instruction and are addressed through micro- and minilessons, writer's notebooks, and conferences. However, students also learn that writers make choices about language use and it is these deliberate choices that set their writing apart.

Though teaching the use of technology has not been a focus in the units described in this book, technology has been a valuable resource for students and teacher. Students have used computers

- to engage in research that draws on library and Internet sources;
- to conduct interviews of individuals geographically distant from themselves;
- to complete multiple drafts of original writing;
- to include multimedia into written papers;
- to complete final products of various types.

They have been encouraged to see technology as a tool and resource that supports active engagement with reading and writing in the world.

Taking a Step Back

The students in this class represent a highly diverse group of individuals (recall the range of grade and performance levels), and Tracy believes that competency in literacy is essential for all students. By placing the emphasis on strategies, processes, and skills, she has worked to create a sense of competence and personal power for each of the students. Her efforts include making these strategies, processes, and skills explicit. She knows that some students will come to know and operationalize these without explicit instruction; others will not. To level the playing field she strives to help all students use strategies, processes, and skills in varying scaffolded contexts in order to help them do so independently later.

Recently, a local teacher lamented how her district has implemented revised state standards at the middle school level, requiring teachers to "cover" units representing all the example genres listed for their grade level. The result? Too little time for students to really gain a deep sense of a given genre before moving on to the next. Coverage is one way to approach curriculum, and unfortunately many districts are unintentionally encouraging this model. As noted earlier, however, though forces external to the classroom often tell us what to do, they generally do not offer guidance on how to do it—and this can be a good thing! Instead of pursuing a coverage model, Tracy has chosen to emphasize the deep connections that transcend genres.

By working with students to examine the ways authors choose genre and use genre to help shape a message; by supporting students as they craft rubrics that capture the essence of a genre, support conversations about the genre, and help them gain an internalized sense of a genre; and by supporting students as they craft texts in genres that may be new or unfamiliar, she has helped them internalize their sense of the possibilities and connections genres offer. By linking nonfiction texts representing various genres and explicitly showing how highly diverse representations might be used to craft similar messages for varying audiences and effects, she has emphasized time and again the range of possibilities and choices authors can access. By demonstrating the connections among major themes that confront us generation after generation through "post-hole" studies, ones that dig deep into important issues, students have an opportunity to understand the power and possibility they possess to enter into the world of ideas through their writing.

Does the model work as a vehicle for realizing the requirements imposed externally? Absolutely. Working from their sense of internalized knowledge of strategies, processes, and skills, students are better equipped to move into other expectations and other unfamiliar genres that may confront them in the form of mandated and recommended external assessments.

10

What About the Growth of the Writer?

Through the semester of writing workshop, students revealed to Tracy what they needed to know as she examined their fastwrites, early drafts, and final papers. By analyzing their writing, she was able to make strategic decisions about instruction. In like fashion—analysis of the students' work at the end of units and in the final portfolio—reveals much about what they have learned and are able to do as a result of the semester's instruction. This information is important to both the student and the teacher. For the student, the ability to think critically about her own work and trace growth builds a sense of power and capability (Mahoney 2002). For the teacher, close analysis of papers provides concrete evidence of student learning and helps her judge which lessons were most effective, which skills and craft lessons have found their way into independent use, which practices have encouraged risk taking, and which aspects of the overall instructional design have yielded an improved sense of self as a writer.

Students have generated an amazing amount of writing during the semester, particularly when all drafts and final papers are included. Not only have they turned in miniportfolios at the conclusion of each unit consisting of all of their fastwrites, drafts, and self-reflections, they have also assembled a comprehensive portfolio that spans the semester. In this end-of-semester portfolio, students include their best works—ones that showcase their skills as writers—as well as a self-reflection that requires them to think about their own growth as a writer across and beyond the semester.

In Chapter 2, four writers were introduced as representative of the range and interests of students in the class. In this chapter, we will revisit each of these students to reflect on their progress. In specific, we are interested in several foci.

- How did attitudes about writing change? Did students write with more enthusiasm? Were they more engaged in their writing? Did they write more as the semester progressed?

139

- Was there evidence of transfer of skills and craft lessons taught in the class to the individual's own writing?
- Finally, what evidence do we see of heightening powers of self-reflection and self-assessment? If there is evidence, what is the impact on the writing? On the student?

Explicating these questions through the lens of student work allows us to consider the effectiveness of various practices and strategies and to think about how they might need to be adjusted. After all, teaching is an organic process, and we are always looking for ways to enhance the instructional environment for our students.

What About Attitudes About Writing?

This semester every student has completed four different attitude surveys and multiple reflections. In addition, selected students have taken part in interviews to gather background information about their writing histories and to chart their development in writing across the semester. Lucas and Lily, both freshmen, and Celly and Stan, both seniors, came into the semester with widely differing skills and attitudes about writing. Lucas, for example, started the semester with lots of reluctance, making it clear up front the impact his learning disability had played in his development as a reader and writer and describing his huge hesitation about sharing his writing. Celly began the semester saying, "I think writing is important. However, I don't enjoy writing, personally. I don't enjoy it mostly because I'm not good at it." Though they differed in terms of their assessment of their writing ability, these two students represent similar attitudes about writing.

In contrast, Lily and Stan represent students who love writing. From the first day Lily says, "I love writing. Sometimes I write merely to finish the work. Which is not so much fun and when my writing is forced it's not as profound, as my mind is elsewhere. But, when I write for myself, it is a wonderful thing." Even at the onset of the class, she is aware of the fact that she prefers writing for herself more than other types of writing, but nonetheless, her investment is high. Stan, on the other hand, loves writing just about everything, and he is immersed sufficiently in writing to recognize his areas of preference. This was made clear in his first survey where he shares, "I like writing, plain and simple. My favorite forms of writing are more towards the creative end of things such as poetry or stories, but when I get started, I have fun with everything."

The challenge for Tracy throughout the semester has been that of building positive engagement with writing leading to positive feelings about writing for all of her students. That means engaging students like Celly and Lucas in developmentally appropriate tasks so that their confidence and competence can continue to develop while also building on the proficiency and enthusiasm of students like Stan and Lily.

The scaffolding provided in the various units has allowed Tracy the opportunity to target specific types of skills and craft lessons to help less proficient writers gain essential skills. Because students moved fluidly from whole class to individual to group work, she has had multiple opportunities to initially teach and then reinforce skills as needed. For some students, this instructional model provided five or more opportunities for specific reteaching of subject matter presented in minilessons using brief individual or small group encounters. For other students for whom the subject matter was either an extension of previous learning or reinforcement, there was less need for this additional content-focused interaction.

At the midpoint in the semester, attitudinal surveys revealed progress. Celly notes that, "Writing is very important. We encounter writing in our daily lives: newspapers, books, TV, etc. . . . It's necessary to know how to write and write it good." Significantly, she is now describing a stronger sense of purpose for writing, framing it within the context of her everyday life. Stan's attitudes about writing have broadened, also. He writes, "I feel writing is *exciting* [emphasis his]. I think it's a great way to convey information, be inspired, express yourself, or just have fun." His enjoyment and interest in writing have not lessened, and he now identifies conveying information as an important reason for writing.

By the end of the semester, surveys and interviews suggest continued growth in positive reaction to writing. Lucas, who entered the semester as one of the most reluctant writers in the class, reflects significant growth. Though still reluctant to share his writing with unknown audiences ("[t]he only people that I am going to show this to [are] you and the person I interviewed"), he shares that, "I would not be opposed to showing it to anyone else that asked." This willingness is a huge leap from his fear of sharing evidenced earlier in the semester. As importantly, he now describes plans to "continue to write over the summer." Celly's enthusiasm is wonderful to read! In her final survey she exclaims, "I think writing is awesome. I learn many unexpected things when I write. For the last paper I wrote I truly learned about myself while writing it." Stan, who entered the semester as one of the strongest and most confidence writers, responds, "I really like writing. I feel like I was exposed to a lot of new things this year and that I am a much more well-rounded writer. I like to express myself with writing." He says in his final survey, "I like to find out what I feel about something. Sometimes, I never really know a subject until I write about it. When I write, I delve into what I really think about it." He is beginning to realize that writing is a process of knowing and discovery.

What About Engagement with Writing?

For all the students, working on topics and genres of their choice provided opportunities for heightened engagement with their own writing and encouraged them to write more and to spend longer periods of time engaged in development of various pieces. Lucas highlights what can happen when a reluctant writer becomes involved with a topic. He described the information gathering that went into the development of his first-choice paper reporting that, "The interviewing process is more difficult than I thought." As he pursued his topic he discovered the need to do a second interview because his first source was not as knowledgeable as needed. Ultimately, he was so pleased with his final paper that he planned to take it back to his source for sharing. By the end of the semester he not only has indicated an interest in writing over the summer, he has identified a desire to "make writing a part of [his] life."

Despite the fact that Lily started the semester with positive feelings about writing, she made it clear in early surveys that writing was easy to put on the back burner. Across the semester, she moved from reporting that

I need to write. I almost never do, and that's really important to me.

to

I like to write, but never really have the time.

to finally,

I love to write!

For Lily and some other students, the option of choice was initially a difficult one. In her final reflection she shared, "When I wrote my first choice piece for Tracy, I had no idea where to start. . . . When there is no one there to tell me things, such as what genre to write in, I am completely lost. Since I had never really written for myself, I didn't know how to just . . . write!" She, like many high school students, require support when given the opportunity to exercise choice, particularly if that option has not been offered to them before. Nonetheless, she thrived in the environment, reporting that, "I also think that, demonstrated in my work, I have no problem writing about what is important to me. It was sort of difficult to turn in some of my work at first, but I got over it quickly."

Beginning the semester as a reluctant writer, Celly reported that she writes "only when I have to for school." By mid-semester her surveys illustrate a shift in her writing patterns. She describes that she writes, "All the time during this class. Sometimes I write at home just for fun and my own enjoyment." In her final portfolio reflection she shares that she now writes, "almost daily." Writing has become a constant feature in her life as she has found multiple personal reasons to make the effort to get her words on paper.

For Stan writing has always been a source of pleasure. His engagement flourished because of the social environment of the workshop. He shares,

> The class itself was full of great people, too, and I had a chance to make some good friends. I am glad you have us sit at different places each day. Sometimes it is easy to fall into patterns and sit with the same people everyday. But I think this just isolates us from the resources around us. I felt like the changing of tables helped us as students to learn more about each other and really bond. Toward the end of the semester, you could really feel the connection between everyone. Another aspect of class that I really enjoyed was the round table. As silly as it sounds, I always looked forward to it for some reason. I guess it was because it gave us a chance to break off from the formalities of the class and just sit, talk, and laugh. Sometimes it is easy to get caught up with the roles of the student and the teacher. But I felt that you saw us at our level and that we all were equal in a way. Because, although you are the real teacher, I think we both teach each other things.

His engagement with other writers within the very personal environment of the workshop allowed him to grow and to help others grow as well.

Was There Evidence of Transfer from Skills and Craft Lessons?

Instruction in sentence structure was a significant feature for all students during the semester as the class as a whole examined examples from outstanding writers and then attempted to import specific characteristics into their own texts. At the beginning of the semester, Tracy and Lucas met to set two large goals for his writing. As they examined early fastwrites, they noted that he tended to create sentences that ranged from short, choppy, simple sentences to ones that ambled on and on. He liked to use more interesting structures, but tended to lose control when he ventured away from controlled simple sentences to ones that used various types of coordination or subordination. Lucas also noted that he was unhappy with the ways his papers started. Together, they established sentence structure and creating interesting leads as two goals for the term.

Lucas's final portfolio abounds with examples of sentences that demonstrate control over compound structures and others that experiment with subordination using dependent clauses. For example, we find, "This is a dangerous game, but the team drew hope from the last game when a member of the opposing side died from tripping on a sock." And from his final self-evaluation we see, "The thing that I am most proud of from this last semester is the piece that was put into the

Communicator. It was fun to write and it is still funny every time I read it. I think I did everything I had planned to do this semester and quite a bit more like improving my literary skills."

The various drafts of papers in his portfolio yield many examples of experimentation with new leads. For example, in earlier drafts of his first free-choice paper he begins with this sentence.

> For this project, I have decided to interview my mom about the September 11th attacks. The reason I chose her was because she was, for the most part the only person that I had access to that has been alive for a historical event and it was 9/11.

By his final draft we find a new lead that captures reader interest quickly.

> The annoying beep! Beep! Beep! Of her alarm clock woke her up. The room was dark and bland. She turned on the radio, the clock lit up, and she heard the DJ talking about how a plane had crashed into the World Trade Center. She got up and walked through the hall with its blue carpet and turned on the news to see what had happened.

Lily started the semester feeling a little overwhelmed with the thought of writing on topics of her own choice. Tracy helped by demonstrating many different ways to enter a piece of writing and by engaging Lily in fastwrites everyday. Lily notes, "I loved the fastwrites. They were able to get my mind revving up. They are excellent. I got tons of ideas from them." By engaging in many different types of fast starts for writing, Lily found she had a wealth of strategies for finding her own topics for future papers.

In her skills sheet Lily had highlighted consistent use of tense, adding details to make paragraphs and sentences more complete, and showing her character's thinking and feelings as three of her goals. As noted, she has good control of writing basics for a freshman. In her final piece she demonstrates skill in each of these areas of focus.

> Angie thrust her leg out, eyes tightly clamped shut, fist clenched, and with one fell swoop, she landed flat on her back, opening her eyes just in time to see the bright red kick ball roll by. She shuffled back to the bench; her eyes fixed on the ground.
> "You should have kept your eyes on the ball."
> Angie turned to Kate, "You should keep your big, fat mouth shut!"
> "Kate," Ms. Peterson's voice shot from the opposite end of the bench, "you're up!"

In many of her writing samples, she demonstrates the types of sentence craft that Tracy emphasized all semester and showcases her strong command of writing craft.

For example, the following excerpt reflects the types of sentences examined and modeled from the works of writers such as Elie Wiesel and Khaled Hosseini.

> Gunfire.
>
> My body flows perfectly into the water. Coming out of my streamline I reach above my head and push my body forward. Again and again I reach for the wall. But as I count the number of laps it only seems to take longer. My lungs tighten, and still I push onward, plunging my face into the water as my hands pull forward.

Twice during the semester, Tracy asked students to write to the same prompt: Tell Me a Story. Celly's first attempt reflects a basic beginning followed by mostly simple sentences that carry her story in predictable ways:

> There is a girl. She's not the prettiest girl, most popular at school or the richest. But she is a nice girl. She's polite and she respects adults. She's also talented. In fact, very talented. She can do so many things so well. Well, except one thing: She can't play sports.
>
> Ever since her childhood, she plays the piano. When she was young, she started and played the piano because her parents made her. All of her piano teachers thought she was just so talented in playing the piano, but she hated it. She dislikes playing the piano because she had to bear hours of practicing. Her play times with friends were taken away . . . just so many thing[s] made her dislike playing the piano . . .

Her later attempt at this prompt reflects growing control over many features that she has been taught this semester.

> Tomorrow is my birthday. Every year I feel so excited at least a week prior to my birthday. But on the actual day, I don't feel anything different. I don't feel a year older. I don't feel the day is as special as how excited I was before. I get presents and I blow out candles, but it's just another day; the clock is ticking just as usual . . .
>
> I begged my sister to go shopping today with me. She agreed. It was great because I can go shopping and buy stuff without having to open up my wallet and take out cash or swipe my credit card. Today, I can just pick and take it to the register, and someone else would take care of the rest.
>
> We walked around the mall, peeking in at the stores through the window as we passed by each entrance. No store seemed to have a special promotion. "It's my special day tomorrow, but no special promotions?" I thought. Everything seemed so normal. I feel like they should offer me great deals, but it didn't happen.
>
> As we entered Lord & Taylor, the shoe racks caught my eyes. We rushed to the rack that was labeled "size 8," and pushed ourselves through a crowd of

people that was there before we arrived. Moving eyes quickly, I skimmered through the entire rack as I picked the ones that mostly made my eyes sparkle. Feeling rich with all of the shoes in the small area made by my left arm and chest, I rushed to a chair. I opened all the boxes and tried the shoes on. This was the best part; I felt like a Cinderella as the prince handed me the shoe to try to see if it fit . . .

If we analyze the second selection we find

- more development of text
- a more interesting lead
- attempts to create a context
- multiple characters
- alternation of sentence lengths and types
- introductory words, phrases, and clauses
- correct and informative use of proper nouns
- experimentation with styles (see the Sandra Cisneros quality of "but it's just another day; the clock is ticking just as usual . . ."
- references to other pieces of literature ("I felt like a Cinderella as the prince handed me the shoe . . .")
- use of precise words to carry meaning (swiped my credit card, peeking in stores, special promotions)

Even in the case of her invented word "skimmered" we find a usage that adds interest to the piece.

By the end of the semester, we find impressive control beginning to appear in Celly's writing. For example, in the following character below we are able to sense much about the character's personality that lurks behind the words.

Natalia walks home exhausted but thinking about the next two days off excites her. No plans yet but she knows well that she'll be kept busy all through the two freebies. Even if nothing is written under those two dates in her impeccable schedule, she knows she'll at least have one thing to do: cleaning the house. Again.

She doesn't know since when, but she has become a clean freak. Her studio is clean and spotless; it never has one particle of dust roaming around the floor. Again, Natalia steps inside her wooden door and conscientiously hangs her keys on the hook instead of throwing them on the sofa along with her purse.

She changes her outfit as soon as she comes home. The reason is that, first of all, her everyday outfit is quite uncomfortable after wearing it all day. Holding a job as a model, she wants to dress well even if she's not on a fashion show. Many photographers, producers, editors, and even ordinary people roving around the streets of NYC recognize her. Most of the time she wears high heels and perfectly matching outfits, which looks good, silhouetting her perfectly shaped body, but it can also be very uncomfortable. Secondly, she hates the feeling of wearing the clothes she has worn outside of the house. She feels the outside germs traveling from her clothes to her furniture as she sits, leans, and consistently makes acquaintances with them.

Celly's sentence variation—both type of sentences used and length—as well as her use of details, choice of specific words, and infusion of voice combine to create a character sketch that not only reflects much of her work across the semester but also a piece that leaves the reader wanting more.

As a strong writer, Stan has worked this semester to hone his ability to paint a picture with words using very precise vocabulary and carefully crafted sentences to create an effect for his reader.

> The boat motor made a low gurgling noise as it pushed us through the cool aquamarine depths of Georgian Bay. The sun beat down on our young backs, climbing down our shirts and warming us to our bones. I could taste the aroma of gasoline and sunscreen on my tongue as we left a thin trail of white blue-gray smoke in the air behind us. I looked up as the wind brushed the hair from my eyes to see two friends sitting together. One was my brother Ben and the other was our good friend Riley. Both held fishing poles tightly in their hands and laughed as we hit another wave which sent a fine spray of water over the hull of the boat. As we approached the little island we slowed and changed from a gurgle to a mere burble before stopping completely.

An excerpt from a longer piece that he titled "A Day in the Life of Our Beautiful Buoyant Bay Boat," this description relies on carefully chosen vocabulary (low gurgling noise, aquamarine depths, aroma of gasoline and sunscreen, thin trail of white blue-gray smoke, changed from a gurgle to a mere burble) and skillfully crafted sentences to place the reader directly into the text.

The types of skills and craft lessons that were taught and that found their way into each of the students' writing will serve them well as they move into new writing situations and into new genres. Even for writing that occurs in test situations where choice of neither topic nor genre may be available, confidence and skill in importing the types of writing features demonstrated by these representative students will be of enormous benefit.

What About Self-Reflection and Self-Assessment?

One of Tracy's major goals for the semester was to help students develop abilities to think critically about their writing, to determine areas of strength and identify areas for continued work. After each major paper and in the final portfolio, students were asked to craft reflections that assessed their progress in relation to the goals they had set for their writing. As a reluctant writer, Lucas entered the semester worrying about basic writing skills such as spelling and punctuation. Throughout the semester, minilessons and conferences focused on helping him to build these skills. In his final evaluation, he describes his own perceptions of his accomplishments in these areas.

> The spelling and grammar in this essay are very good. I used spell check and other resources to correct any mistakes. Punctuation is the same as spelling and grammar. I did not have a whol lot of dialogue and that is probably this paper's biggest weekness. I did express my true feelings about this topic and I feel that I was very honist. The strengths of my paper are pretty murch it is long and pretty well developed with lots of feeling and no mistakes. [spelling errors in original]

As an example of first-draft writing, the reflection still demonstrates a few concerns about spelling. Nonetheless, it also shows that Lucas is now able to look at his work with a critical eye, identifying the areas where he has gained success through the exercise of specific resources. Moreover, he demonstrates his knowledge of the importance of writing with feeling and honesty, of adequately developing a topic to support reader understanding, and of being able to carefully edit his work to support clear communication of his message.

As a part of her self-evaluation, Lily has chosen to use the checklist developed by the class to review her final paper. In her final review of her nonfiction choice piece she checked for the use of

- metaphors
- writing with a purpose and a developed theme
- feelings of an individual or larger group of people
- powerful imagery
- descriptive words
- dramatic sentences and paragraphs (varying short/long for a purpose)
- repetition of words and phrases for effect
- parallel sentence structure
- history told through a personal account (use of first-person, third-person, or third-person omniscient point of view)
- powerful lines with deeper meaning that inspire reflection and introspection about humanity
- points in the writing that go beyond the text
- control of spelling, grammar, and usage
- varied punctuation (including use of commas, periods, quotes, semicolons, hyphens, dashes, colons, question marks, and exclamation points)

Not only is she able to identify examples in her own writing that illustrate her ability to use these features, but also the degree to which she was able to use them. This suggests far more than surface knowledge, and this deeper understanding will serve her well in new writing contexts in the future.

For a student who came into the semester with reticence about her writing, Celly's final self-reflections illustrate a keen awareness of the role of the literature that has surrounded her all semester as a major influence on her writing.

> Different things taught in class, such as quick writes, skills, *Night* by Elie Wiesel, were amazingly a big help for me when it came to writing. First of all, I will share my experience with *Night*. Reading *Night* with the class before the nonfiction assignment was a great idea because I learned what true nonfiction was. I also wrote my nonfiction story based on a true war, the Korean War. The experience Wiesel had to go through was much different from the ones my characters had to experience. However, because both works were based on wars, I was able to find similar ideas and use Wiesel's writing to make mine as interesting. For example, I was able to understand my characters' feelings through Wiesel's writing. I felt they felt the same way. Worries, anxiety, misery . . . Also, the thing that I learned the most from reading *Night* was using various sentence structures. Wiesel was definitely a master at writing really short sentences, short sentences, medium length, long sentences, really long sentences . . . I learned that varying sentences create a beautiful pace to the writing, and I decided to use that to catch my readers. It was a success!

Not only did the literature chosen for the semester successfully support Celly's development of sentence and paragraph structures in her own writing, it also allowed her to think about her own topics in different ways. Initially, she expressed strong reservations about nonfiction. However, as she became engaged in her first nonfiction piece, she became totally involved relating the story of her grandmother. The connections that she made to the literature being studied, and particularly to the dramatic and horrific account in *Night*, allowed her to think about her own content in ways that assisted her in coming to terms with the emotions and feelings of her characters.

Of significance for Celly was the growing sense of pride and satisfaction that she feels about her writing across the semester. She shares,

> I have to say that I'm proud of every single work done in class. I loved how every piece turned out. Even until now, after a semester of writing class, I'm still weak at writing. I still don't write the best papers. I still can't write something that could be published and win prizes. However, I love each and every one of my works. They all mean something different to me. I wrote them with my best ability and even though they aren't perfect, I'm proud that I've written those!

Celly still is driven to be perfect—to produce the perfect paper. And, she understands that her work still is not perfect. However, she now has a sense of progress and a pathway to pursue.

> I believe that if I just hold on to the passion I have right now for writing, I could write the "perfect" paper one day. I'm still a learner. I think there's so much to learn about writing. One semester of writing class is not going to make me the best writer ever, but this semester has taught me how to make writing come alive with zeal. So if I just continue to hold this interest and favor for writing, then I'm sure I'll improve more and more. Thank you so much for introducing me to the beauty of writing.

She also demonstrates a keen understanding of her own process, her own promise, and her own probable steps to continue growing as a writer.

Stan, too, has grown in his ability to think about and discuss his own writing. Though his skills and interests were strong initially, he reports at the end of the semester that "this was the first year where I really got good lessons in all the technicalities of writing. Although at first it did not seem all that exciting, those are very necessary and important tools to know." As already described, Stan understands the importance of the community in the classroom. He also notes the importance of being pushed beyond his own comfort zone.

> It was very interesting to look at my portfolio and see the different ways I had progressed over the year. I think I matured as a writer and this class helped me do it. I tried to push myself to write outside of my comfort zone, and a lot of the assignments that you provided in class helped me to do that.

Whether the students entered with positive attitudes or negative ones, whether their skills were polished or rough, whether they saw themselves as writers or not, the workshop setting appears to have afforded opportunities for all to develop and use skills with increasing independence and with a heightened sense of awareness of how to craft and sculpt their writing in various genres to create desired effects. As a result, students leave with increased confidence and competence in their writing.

11

How Does Workshop Work for the Teacher?

Tracy expects her students to continuously engage in writing and self-reflection. It is only fitting, therefore, that this narrative about her classroom closes with a reflection from her. It is important to note that Tracy, though young in her career, is not a new teacher. Her professional development experiences with a national writing project site, her continuous study of English language arts content and pedagogy, her prior experiences in the classroom, and her own willingness to think hard about her practice all contributed to create the moment when she decided to seek a confidant who would work alongside her to distill the core values of a workshop classroom and then to translate those values into workable practice for her diverse group of students. This book has narrated the story of what happened along the way. Now, we'll hear the final evaluation from Tracy.

From Teacher-centric to Workshop

I spent my first three years of teaching leaving school at 8:00 in the evening or later every night, toting a rolling luggage rack stacked with journals and notebooks. There simply wasn't enough time in the day to get through all of the student work before I left for the day. I wanted to read and respond to every page; after all, I was the teacher and, therefore, the student's sole responder. I started off my career completely teacher-centric, thinking that I provided everything to my students. I was the bearer of all knowledge and they needed my pages of response to teach them new skills or reaffirm ones they already knew.

It wasn't until years later that I realized I did not have to be my students sole responder; in fact, it was better when they had multiple people to respond to them and in different ways. I realized this from a journalism class that I taught several years into my teaching career. The students in this class knew that they were writing for an audience of over 1,000, so their need for my response was far different than that which I typically gave to my traditional English students. At that time, in my English classes, students would generally do a rough draft and then a final draft, which they would turn in for comments and a grade. The rough draft for these students was a partial or rough complete draft, intended for me to see where they were going, to make sure they were on the right track, and to get them started on their paper so they didn't procrastinate until the night before it was due.

In contrast, my journalism students sought response from their peers in our peer editing sessions, in our newspaper critiques, from students and teachers who read their published article in the paper, and from people who were moved to write a letter to the editor. This response was real, and the authenticity of the response changed the student's motivation to write well and allowed me to move into the role of editor who helped the writers to think about their work in new ways.

My job was to get students to think about the questions they hadn't thought about yet. I would ask them questions such as, Did you get the other side of the story? Is this quote exact? Did you fact check? Are there any legality issues? How do you think that people are going to react? What is your intention in writing this? Yes, I also looked for the nitty-gritty: the misspelled words, than/then, here/hear, and the ever-present its/it's. However, much of the nitty-gritty was also taken care of in peer editing sessions; interestingly, the number of errors in my journalism class was significantly fewer than in my writing classes where I was the dominant audience.

Largely because of this experience, I came to understand the power of audience and ownership as mechanisms for change in student writing. This became a new algorithm: increase the audience and personal ownership, and the writing improves. It works that way for most things. Over the years many students have said they would turn in a paper to a teacher without going through it with a fine-tooth comb; however, when the paper was going to their peers or to an audience of their choice, the writing had to be perfect. It would be embarrassing for their work to go out into the public eye with spelling and grammatical errors.

As I contemplated bringing core workshop values into my writing classes, this history framed my decision making. The first way that I expanded students' audience was with Friday Reading Jams, weekly celebrations where students heard the emerging work of their peers. Students wrote knowing that they could share their work in this forum. They heard work from their peers that inspired them in their own writing. In the Reading Jams students chose when and what they wanted to share. Though there was always the expectation that students would share, no one was forced to move to the author's chair.

After each student read her work, we wrote letters to her about the piece. The members of the student audience wrote about what the piece reminded them of; about words, phrases, and sentences that they loved; about particular connections to events or other pieces of literature. As the semester advanced, these letters became personal and a vehicle for students who would otherwise not talk to get to know each other in this unique dialogue.

After a student read his work to the class, he would have notes from twenty-seven peer responders—not just a review from me. This response became a learning experience not only for the student sharing work, but for all of those responding to it as the note writing encouraged active listening and helped students recognize qualities of good writing. It let the writer know exactly how his or her writing affected others, an immediate response that helped reinforce the value of their writing. In many ways this form of response increased student responsibility and helped to keep my response load manageable. Students earned credit/no credit points for reading at the Reading Jam and for writing letters to their peers.

Building Audience, Increasing Individualization, Decreasing the Teacher Load

In the workshop I move from the role of teacher in front of the class, to peer-advisor-teacher beside the student. In a workshop approach there is time for me to introduce new material to students, as well as work with students individually on skills and mechanics that are thus far unlearned. In my high school classroom, I have students writing at the college level, but I also have students who are unable to recognize what makes a sentence complete. When skills have been missed along the way, students need me to sit down next to them and work one-on-one. They need to be able to ask what they would call "a stupid question" that they simply won't ask in front of the class.

In the move to workshop, the question that drove instruction was "What do my students need?" To become the literate people that I wanted them to become, they needed time to develop as readers and writers. They needed to make choices about their writing. They needed response and feedback. They needed guidance—direct and indirect. The trick was trying to figure out how to give them these things, while maintaining my sanity and my family life.

I have created a number of "staples" that hold the workshop together; these have been described in action in the preceding chapters and include the writer's notebook, which includes a skills and craft section; mini- and microlessons; personalized sheets for recording skills and individual writing goals; reflections; book recommendations; and individual State of the Class sheets for each student. These staples provide consistency, clear objectives, and expectations. They help us move forward through the semester. When I was without this structure in the past, workshop would take on an unwieldy life of itself—with little record of the path it took. I need structure so the students and I can document where we have been and set goals for where we are going. In the structure I can make sure that I am focusing on necessary curricular materials and tracking my work with individual students to be sure they are getting the individualized help they need.

When I didn't have the staples for high school workshop, handling the individualization was difficult. It felt as if I had thirty different classes going on each hour. Although exciting in its organic nature, this level of spontaneity proved to be ultimately unsustainable. The staples developed out of need, and they support individualization of specific goals, strategies, and content; nonetheless, all students are engaged in the same genre-focused work. This consistency allows me to teach to high standards for all students, keep track of everything, and support individual needs. For example, on a skills sheet, one student may be working on writing compound/complex sentences and the other on subject/verb agreement. When I grade the papers, my job becomes more defined because the skills sheet, which students turn in with every paper, helps focus the student's proofreading and direct my comments. The student is responsible for editing his own work for the skills presented in minilessons or individual conferences. The skills sheet focuses my response and grading and helps me track how the student is moving forward in his writing.

Some of my students have gone year after year making the same errors. Basic writers sometimes have an overwhelming and daunting task when asked to improve their writing. Targeting particular areas for focus, breaking skills down for them, and adding these to their skills sheet allows them to improve one skill at a time within the context of their own writing. Their skills need time to marinate as they move toward independent use in their writing.

At the beginning of my teaching career I did one-shot grading. I would assign an essay; students would write the essay; I would grade it and make corrections. Students would get it back, look at the grade, sometimes read the corrections, and stuff it in their folder. Then they would proceed to make the same errors on the next paper. There was no time for corrections, which I address now with the skills sheet. I don't want to spend my time correcting the same errors on student papers over and over.

If I have a student who is in tenth grade and writes four-page stories with three paragraphs, specific skills expectations for crafting paragraphs will be added to the skills sheet of their notebook. We'll go over these notes together, either in a whole class minilesson or an individual session depending on student need. The next time the student turns in a final draft, I look over the skills sheet to see which areas we've agreed are ones for focus. If I see again that this student hasn't worked on crafting correct paragraphs, the paper goes back to him for a *redo*. I don't spend the time going through the piece until I see that the student has first done his job as his own editor. I have spent too much of my time correcting things that students should be empowered and expected to self-correct. Giving students the responsibility as their first editor actually forces them to accept responsibility for making their writing stronger.

Other mechanisms helped, too. At the beginning of each class period, students respond to a writing invitation and then move into their own independent writing. As I move from individual to individual around the classroom, I read each student's writing invitation, talk to the student about it, offer observations about the content of the piece, reinforce some aspect of skills or craft use, and give them up to ten points for their work. This brief discussion also provides the time for me to touch base with each of them about the writing under development. Some days these conferences are very short, while other days I spend up to ten minutes with one student.

I start off my conferences by asking students to raise their hand if they need to see me right away. If there are many students who need to see me, I query as to whether it is a quick question and then I address those students first. That way I can move about the room and get to the students who need me the most first. I strive to read all of my students' fastwrites during the hour. This, again, gives them immediate feedback, and it gives me a time to conference one-on-one. Some evaluation has moved from being the isolated acts that I use to do early on Saturday mornings and late almost every night to interactive conferences face-to-face with my students.

Sure, I still do some responding and grading by myself. But it is much less of a burden, and it is typically grading final drafts of papers that I already know well from the many times I have seen drafts in class. When I see a final draft, it isn't the first time that I am seeing the piece. Sometimes I have seen it stem out of a writing invitation and then move through several drafts before it is turned in for a final grade. The result is invariably better quality work.

In my teaching, I came to a point where I had to think about what I was assuming responsibility for that I should be expecting students to take responsibility for. When I shifted my teaching to include structures that allowed students to take "guided" responsibility for their work, my own workload evolved from being full of tedious grading to being a collaborator and guide in students' learning processes.

The student's self-evaluation letter is a highly important tool. In this letter students write in detail about their strengths and weaknesses. I can agree or disagree with them and point out additional insight about their work and learning. However, with my comments I am not starting from scratch. I have the students own insights from which to work. This accomplishes two things: First it makes my job easier, and second, it makes the student's job more difficult in a meaningful way. Students will often start their self-evaluation letter only to realize that they need to go back and make changes to their final draft. In this way, these letters serve as a tool for editing as well as evaluation.

My goal is to get students to see their own strengths and weaknesses so they can develop a critical eye for their own work. I have found this to be a necessary skill that I needed to teach my students to help them develop as writers. They are not going to be with me for the rest of their writing careers, so my comments alone can only take them so far. I must help them develop their self-evaluation skills and in doing so will help them become better editors and writers.

Final Thoughts

I've found juggling the demands of a teacher to be intense. Teachers are expected to create curriculum, evaluate students, attend school and district meetings, pursue staff development and continuing education, take parent phone calls in and out of school, respond to parent and student emails, be there for students during lunch and after school, and the list goes on. I am a mother of two young children, and when my second was born I knew that something had to give. This is when I started asking myself big questions: What am I doing that I don't need to do? What can I delegate to my students and what effects will that have on me and on them?

What I've done is cut out the things that didn't matter. For example, I used to collect students' writing invitations every night and write comments on them. Now, I read them as part of our conferences during class, and I mark them into my grade book at that time. The only time that they are turned in is when I do a notebook check every other week. When I answered these big questions for myself, I ended up refining my practice so that there were more conferences in class and more one-on-one interaction with me. The workload for the students increased when I gave up the control that I had held for too many years. In return, I have a manageable paper-grading load, and I can focus my energy on giving the students what they need to keep writing as much as they can write.

When I stopped planning activity after activity, focus shifted from activities to students and developing true and meaningful curriculum for them. Focusing on my students and their needs gives me a continual source of energy. Instead of teaching lessons, I started teaching students. Teenagers are full of energy, and I've found a workshop approach channels this energy into our classrooms in meaningful, sustainable, and manageable ways.

The big question whenever teachers try something new or fine-tune their practice is "Does it work?" I have found that this approach does work for me. It was liberating to find that I could both lessen the grading load that I carried while at the same time improve instruction and give students more responsibility for their learning. It is more exciting for me to work on the curriculum that will help students become the critical writers that I want them to be.

In my teaching I am continuously evolving and changing how I do things. However, what is constant is that I am committed to creating a classroom community where students are valued and where there are high expectations that they will have an active role in their own education. I don't want to take the responsibility for correcting student's errors again and again, because each time I do, I am taking away their responsibility for their own work.

I wouldn't go back to the traditional type of teaching that I did in my early years. Why? Because that approach left too many of my students unengaged and left behind; they didn't grow as readers and writers. Why? Because it was too labor intensive for me, and the labor involved did not typically lead to student growth as readers and writers. The time I spent buried under papers was time I could not spend planning and envisioning curriculum to engage my students.

I obviously opted to change my teaching style. Workshop allows me to share ownership with students while still giving them the guidance and direct and indirect instruction that they need. I will continue to look for ways to give students more responsibility over their learning. Workshop is never stagnant, which is what keeps the energy in it for me as a teacher. It continues to evolve —with each day that we write, with each paper that we conference, and with each group of students that walks into my room. I can't foresee where workshop will "end up"; I can foresee that it will continue to change with each new group of students.

NCTE Beliefs and Standards

NCTE Beliefs About the Teaching of Writing, November 2004

Just as the nature of and expectation for literacy has changed in the past century and a half, so has the nature of writing. Much of that change has been due to technological developments—from pen and paper, to typewriter, to word processor, to networked computer, to design software capable of composing words, images, and sounds. These developments not only expanded the types of texts that writers produce, they also expanded immediate access to a wider variety of readers. With full recognition that writing is an increasingly multifaceted activity, we offer several principles that should guide effective teaching practice.

1. Everyone has the capacity to write, writing can be taught, and teachers can help students become better writers.
2. People learn to write by writing.
3. Writing is a process.
4. Writing is a tool for thinking.
5. Writing grows out of many different purposes.
6. Conventions of finished and edited texts are important to readers and therefore to writers.
7. Writing and reading are related.
8. Writing has a complex relationship to talk.
9. Literate practices are embedded in complicated social relationships.
10. Composing occurs in different modalities and technologies.
11. Assessment of writing involves complex, informed, human judgment. (full document available at www.ncte.org)

National Council of Teachers of English/International Reading Association Standards

1. Students read a wide range of print and non-print texts to build an understanding of texts, of themselves, and of the cultures of the United States and the world; to acquire new information; to respond to the needs and demands of society and the workplace; and for personal fulfillment. Among these texts are fiction and nonfiction, classic and contemporary works.

2. Students read a wide range of literature from many periods in many genres to build an understanding of the many dimensions (e.g., philosophical, ethical, aesthetic) of human experience.

3. Students apply a wide range of strategies to comprehend, interpret, evaluate, and appreciate texts. They draw on their prior experience, their interactions with other readers and writers, their knowledge of word meaning and of other texts, their word identification strategies, and their understanding of textual features (e.g., sound-letter correspondence, sentence structure, context, graphics).

4. Students adjust their use of spoken, written, and visual language (e.g., conventions, style, vocabulary) to communicate effectively with a variety of audiences and for different purposes.

5. Students employ a wide range of strategies as they write and use different writing process elements appropriately to communicate with different audiences for a variety of purposes.

6. Students apply knowledge of language structure, language conventions (e.g., spelling and punctuation), media techniques, figurative language, and genre to create, critique, and discuss print and non-print texts.

7. Students conduct research on issues and interests by generating ideas and questions, and by posing problems. They gather, evaluate, and synthesize data from a variety of sources (e.g., print and non-print texts, artifacts, people) to communicate their discoveries in ways that suit their purpose and audience.

8. Students use a variety of technological and information resources (e.g., libraries, databases, computer networks, video) to gather and synthesize information and to create and communicate knowledge.

9. Students develop an understanding of and respect for diversity in language use, patterns, and dialects across cultures, ethnic groups, geographic regions, and social roles.

10. Students whose first language is not English make use of their first language to develop competency in the English language arts and to develop understanding of content across the curriculum.

11. Students participate as knowledgeable, reflective, creative, and critical members of a variety of literacy communities.

12. Students use spoken, written, and visual language to accomplish their own purposes (e.g., for learning, enjoyment, persuasion, and the exchange of information).

(full document available at www.ncte.org)

Tools

State of the Class

Student Name: _____

	Monday	Tuesday	Wednesday	Thursday	Friday
Week of _____					
Week of _____					
Week of _____					
Week of _____					

Note: One form for each student.

Writing Workshop Record

Complete the following information for all of your rough and final draft writing. Keep this record stapled in your reader's/writer's notebook.

Date	Subject of piece	Title	Genre	Draft number	Publication/audience options

Syllabus and Expectations for
Reading and Writing Workshop

*Most of the basic material a writer works with is acquired before
the age of fifteen.*

—Willa Cather

Syllabus

Dear Student,

Welcome! I am anxious to embark on this writing journey together. Along the way we will learn a lot about ourselves, each other, and writing. In our workshop there are four aspects that are essential: time, ownership, response, and community.

Time

You will be given time in class to write and you will be expected to do so. I can't quite explain the feeling that will fill the room when everyone is working on a piece of writing. I can simply say that it is powerful and inspires me to write more. Class time is precious. Sometimes the class will be completely silent while people are working on their pieces. When we are in quiet writing time, it is essential that the room is quiet. Often when writers are working and another student starts talking the writers "lose" their words. It boils down to respecting everyone in the room. When we are sharing and discussing work excellent conversations tend to fill the room.

Ownership

You should care about the writing that you do in this course. If you don't, then more than likely you are not writing about topics that matter to you. Of course you are writing to fill the expectations of this class, but you should also be writing for yourself. When students write for themselves their writing naturally improves. We write for different reasons: to dream, to inspire, to understand, and to explore. Find your reason to write.

Response

During this course we will respond to our writing in various ways. Sometimes we will meet in small groups and share our pieces. Sometimes we will read one piece as an entire class. We will write letters to our peers about the pieces that they share. The goal of response is not to tear writing to shreds; it should make the writer want to write more.

Community

In our workshop, community is essential. I expect you to take risks in your writing. I know from my own experience that when I take risks in my writing sometimes it works and sometimes it doesn't. What is essential is the learning that happens during that exploration process. Our writing community will support taking risks.

During this course we will be developing as writers as well as people. All of us are starting at different levels and we have different backgrounds. We each have a voice that will enrich the class. Do everything that you can do to encourage and support your fellow writers. Again, it boils down to respect. I expect the best from you.

What Is Workshop?

Workshop happens when students practice writing as the central activity in the classroom. You will be given *time* to write and will be *expected* to do so. You will also be expected to select topics, sources, and genres (i.e., short story, poem, persuasive essay, etc.) for your writing. The structure of workshop includes whole class instruction when we will explore new ideas and skills together, as well as a lot of time to apply these ideas and skills to your writing experiences.

Expectations at a Glance

I expect you to be in class on time and ready to work. Work missed due to an unexcused absence may not be made up and will affect the outcome of the grade.

I will present minilessons that address structural, grammatical, and technical areas of writing. I develop my minilessons to fit class needs. You are expected to keep notes and apply the information to your writing.

You will compose multiple pages of writing every week. Your work will add up quickly. Be sure to keep everything you write organized. Everything that you write is part of your writing history. **You must keep all of your work during the semester.** If you don't the end of the quarter could be a sad day when you don't

164

have anything in your portfolio. You will have an intense and blissful time creating your portfolio. We'll talk more about this later.

Materials for Writing Workshop

>   folder or three-ring binder
>   pens and pencils (for writing everyday)
>   spiral-bound notebook

Please contact me if any of these items will be difficult to obtain.

Grading

You will be assessed through a combination of portfolio assessment, ongoing teacher and student self-evaluation, quizzes, daily assignments, writing assignments, and participation. Late work and class work missed due to an unexcused absence is not accepted. To earn participation points, you obviously must be in class to participate. If you are tardy, you will lose some of your daily participation points.

Late Work

In the past I have found that students who don't turn an assignment in on time either don't ever turn it in or have not done their best to turn it in on time. I expect you to turn your work in on time. Keep an open line of communication with me if there are extenuating circumstances. Late work will be marked down two letter grades.

Class Rules

We will work together on a basis of mutual respect. I expect you to conduct yourself in an adult manner, to be on time to class, and to be prepared everyday to do your best work.

An Invitation

If you ever have any questions, concerns, or ideas about our class discuss them with me. I enjoy working with students individually so be sure to contact me if you need extra help. I am always anxious to hear your perspective and ideas. Together we can make our class wonderful. I look forward to an engaging semester of learning together.

Expectations for Writing

- Come to class on time every day ready to write. Leave only if it is an emergency. Always let me know where you are going.
- Write between five to ten pages every week.
- Bring a piece to final draft every other week for Thursday Reading Jams.
- Reflect on strengths and weaknesses of specific pieces of writing.
- Apply craft and mechanic lessons from class to writing.
- Keep craft and mechanic lessons and notes organized chronologically in your reader's/writer's notebook.
- Maintain a table of contents in your notebook so you can easily find information.
- Strive to write using correct grammar, spelling and mechanics.
- Explore and make choices about genres.
- Have peer and teacher conferences that focus on specific aspects of your writing generated from your own questions, curiosities, and concerns.
- Find powerful and meaningful subjects to write about.
- Spend at least one hour per week writing outside of class.
- Attempt professional publication.
- Come to class on time and ready to write and be a positive member of our writing community.
- Share work in small and large groups.
- Read in our class Reading Jams.
- Give thoughtful feedback to peers about their work.
- Get to know and work well with your peers.
- Complete all class assignments.
- Keep all of your work organized throughout the semester.
- Maintain a working portfolio in the classroom. When you finish a final draft, paperclip it to your rough drafts, your self-reflection/evaluation, rubric, peer letters, and conference sheets. File it in your working portfolio. Update the writing record inside of your portfolio whenever you add pieces.
- Learn how to use writing resources in the room.
- Maintain a writing record with all of your pieces of writing.
- Keep and use a skills sheet to help you as you edit your work.
- Do everything that you can do to further your own growth as a writer, as well as those around you.
- Respect the writing space in the classroom and do nothing to disturb other's writing.

Expectations for Reading

- Read whole class and individual novels.
- Select novels that are interesting, appropriate, and challenging for you.
- Dedicate at least thirty minutes three times per week outside of class to reading.
- Use "Reading Bliss" time to read your book in class.
- Write reactions to your reading in your writer's notebook. Write a minimum of one page per week.
- As you are reading, become a student of writing.
- Share your reading with the class through book talks.
- Apply minilessons from class to your reading.
- Keep notes from minilessons organized in your reader's/writer's notebook.
- Take excellent care of the books that you borrow from our classroom library. Return them as soon as you are done with them.
- Respect the time and space given to read, enjoy, and study literature.
- Use reading as a way to better understand our world, yourself, and writing.

Works Cited

Allen, Janet. 1995. *It's Never Too Late: Leading Adolescents to Lifelong Literacy*. Portsmouth, NH: Heinemann.

———. 1999. *Words, Words, Words: Teaching Vocabulary in Grades 4–12*. York, ME: Stenhouse.

Allington, Richard L. 2005. "Urgency and Instructional Time." *Reading Today* 23 (1):17.

Anders, Patty, and N. S. Levine. 1990. "Accomplishing Change in Reading Programs." In *Reading in the Middle School*, ed. Gerald Duffy, 77–117. Newark, DE: International Reading Association.

Andrade, Heidi Goodrich. 2003. Rubrics and Self Assessment Project. Accessed 18 January, 2006. Project Zero: Harvard University. www.pz.harvard.edu/Research/RubricSelf.htm.

Andrasick, Kathleen Dudden. 1990. *Opening Texts: Using Writing to Teach Literature*. Portsmouth, NH: Heinemann.

Appleman, Deborah. 2000. *Critical Encounters in High School English: Teaching Literary Theory to Adolescents*. New York: Teachers College Press.

Atwell, Nancie. 1987. *In the Middle: Writing, Reading, and Learning with Adolescents*. Portsmouth, NH: Boynton/Cook Heinemann.

———. 1991. *Workshop 3 by and for Teachers: The Politics of Process*. Portsmouth, NH: Heinemann.

———. 1998. *In the Middle: New Understanding About Writing, Reading, and Learning*. Portsmouth, NH: Heinemann.

Bangert-Drowns, Robert L., Chen-Lin Kulik, and James S. Kulik. 1991. "The Instructional Effect of Feedback in Test-like Events." *Review of Educational Research* 61: 213–38.

Beers, Kylene. 2003. *When Kids Can't Read: What Teachers Can Do*. Portsmouth, NH: Heinemann.

Bennett, Jay. 1990. *Sing Me a Death Song*. New York: Ballantine Books.

———. 1994. *I Never Said I Loved You*. New York: Avon Books.

Blau, Sheridan D. 2003. *The Literature Workshop: Teaching Texts and Their Readers*. Portsmouth, NH: Heinemann.

Bomer, Randy. 1995. *Time for Meaning: Crafting Literate Lives in Middle and High School.* Portsmouth, NH: Heinemann.

Britton, James, Tony Burgess, Nancy Martin, Alex McLeod, and Harold Rosen. 1975. *The Development of Writing Abilities (11–18).* London: Macmillan Education.

Bullock, Richard, ed. 1998. *Why Workshop: Changing Course in 7–12 English.* York, ME: Stenhouse.

Butler, Deborah, and Phillip Winne. 1995. "Feedback and Self-regulated Learning: A Theoretical Synthesis." *Review of Educational Research* 65 (3): 245–81.

Calkins, Lucy. 1983. *Lessons from a Child: On the Teaching and Learning of Writing.* Portsmouth, NH: Heinemann.

Cameron, Julia. 1992. *The Artist's Way: A Course in Discovering and Recovering Your Creative Self.* New York: G. P. Putnam's Sons.

———. 2004. *The Sound of Paper.* New York: G. P. Putnam's Sons.

Daniels, Harvey, and Marilyn Bizar. 1998. *Methods That Matter: Six Structures for Best Practice Classrooms.* York, ME: Stenhouse.

Daniels, Harvey, Steven Zemelman, and Arthur Hyde. 1993. *Best Practice: New Standards for Teaching and Learning in America's Schools.* York, ME: Stenhouse.

———. 1998. *Methods That Matter: Six Structures for Best Practice Classrooms.* York, ME: Stenhouse.

Early, Margaret. 1960. "Stages of Growth in Literary Appreciation." *English Journal* 49 (3): 161–67.

Fleischer, Cathy. 2005, September. Writing Rejuvenation Conference. Eastern Michigan Writing Project.

Fleischer, Cathy, and David Schaafsma. 1998. *Literacy and Democracy: Teacher Research and Composition Studies in Pursuit of Habitable Spaces.* Urbana, IL: National Council of Teachers of English.

Fletcher, Ralph. 1994. *I Am Wings: Poems About Love.* New York: Antheneum.

Fox, Mem. 1985. *Wilfrid Gordon McDonald Partridge.* Brooklyn, NY: Kane/Miller.

Gaughan, John. 2001. *Reinventing English: Teaching in the Contact Zone.* Portsmouth, NH: Heinemann.

Gere, Anne Ruggles, Leila Christenbury, and Kelly Sassi. 2005. *Writing on Demand: Best Practices and Strategies for Success.* Portsmouth, NH: Heinemann.

Graves, Donald. 1994. *A Fresh Look at Writing.* Portsmouth, NH: Heinemann.

Harvey, Stephanie. 1998. *Nonfiction Matters: Reading, Writing, and Research in Grades 3–8.* York, ME: Stenhouse.

Harwayne, Shelley. 2001. *Writing Through Childhood: Rethinking Process and Product.* Portsmouth, NH: Heinemann.

Holbrook, Sara. 1998. *Chicks Up Front.* Cleveland, OH: Cleveland State University.

Hosseini, Khaled. 2003. *The Kite Runner.* New York: Riverhead Books.

Lane, Barry. 1993. *After the End: Teaching and Learning Creative Revision.* Portsmouth, NH: Heinemann.

Lattimer, Heather. 2003. *Thinking Through Genre: Units of Study in Reading and Writing Workshop 4–12*. Portland, ME: Stenhouse.

Lortic, Dan. 1975. *School Teacher: A Sociological Study*. Chicago: University of Chicago Press.

Lowery, Lois. 2000. *Gathering Blue*. New York: Dell Laurel-Leaf.

Mahoney, Jim. 2002. *Power and Portfolios: Best Practices for High School Classrooms*. Portsmouth, NH: Heinemann.

Murray, Donald. 1984. *Write to Learn*. New York: Holt, Rinehart and Winston.

National Council of Teachers of English. 2004. NCTE Beliefs About the Teaching of Writing. Accessed 18 January, 2006. Urbana, IL: NCTE. www.ncte.org.

The National Commission on Writing. April 2003. *The Neglected R*. Accessed 18 January, 2006. New York: College Entrance Examination Board. www.collegeboard.org.

Quinn, Daniel. 1992. *Ishmael: An Adventure of the Mind and Spirit*. New York: Bantam.

Rabinowitz, Peter J., and Michael W. Smith. 1998. *Authorizing Readers: Resistance and Respect in the Teaching of Literature*. Urbana, IL: National Council of Teachers of English.

Ray, Katie Wood. 2004. *About the Authors: Writing Workshop with Our Youngest Writers*. Portsmouth, NH: Heinemann.

Redfield, James. 1993. *The Celestine Prophecy*. New York: Warner Books.

Rief, Linda. 1992. *Seeking Diversity: Language Arts with Adolescents*. Portsmouth, NH: Heinemann.

Robinson, Jay. 1990. *Conversations on the Written Word: Essays on Language and Literacy*. Portsmouth, NH: Boynton/Cook Heinemann.

———. 1998. "Literacy and Lived Lives: Reflections on the Responsibilities of Teachers." In *Literacy and Democracy: Teacher Research and Composition Studies in Pursuit of Habitable Spaces*. Urbana, IL: National Council of Teachers of English.

Romano, Thomas. 2000. *Blending Genre, Altering Style: Writing Multigenre Papers*. Portsmouth, NH: Boynton/Cook Heinemann.

Rosenblatt, Louise. 1938, 1976. *Literature as Exploration*. New York: The Modern Language Association of America.

———. 1978. *The Reader, the Text, the Poem: The Transactional Theory of the Literary Work*. Carbondale: Southern Illinois University Press.

Routman, Regie. 1988. *From Literature to Literacy*. Portsmouth, NH: Heinemann.

———. 1991. *Invitations: Changing Teachers and Learners K–12*. Portsmouth, NH: Heinemann.

Rowlands, Kathleen. 1995. Unpublished review. Portsmouth, NH: Heinemann.

Sedaris, David. 2000. *Me Talk Pretty One Day*. New York: Back Bay Books.

Short, Kathy Gnagey, and Kathryn Mitchell Pierce, eds. 1990. *Talking About Books: Creating Literate Communities*. Portsmouth, NH: Heinemann.

Silverstein, Shel. 1964. *The Giving Tree*. New York: Harper Collins.

Sipe, Rebecca Bowers. 2003. *They Still Can't Spell?* Portsmouth, NH: Heinemann.

Steinbeck, John. 1945/1992. *The Pearl*. New York: Penguin Books.

Stock, Gregory. 1987. *The Book of Questions*. New York: Workman.

Strickland, Kathleen, and James Strickland. 1998. *Reflections on Assessment: Its Purposes, Methods, & Effects on Learning.* Portsmouth, NH: Heinemann.

Teen metaphors. Accessed 18 January, 2006. www.jumbojoke.com/000398.html.

Volavkova, Hana, ed. 1993. *I Never Saw Another Butterfly. Children's Drawings and Poems from Terezin Concentration Camp, 1942–1944.* Revised and expanded by the United States Holocaust Memorial Museum. New York: Schocken Books.

Wiesel, Elie. 1960. *Night.* New York: Hill and Wang/Bantam.

Yagelski, Robert P. 2000. *Literacy Matters: Writing and Reading the Social Self.* New York: Teachers College Press.

Index